MW01241416

PRAISE FOR *THE CUTTLEFISH MARKETER*

"The five essential traits of marketing that Scott and Ivan have laid out in this fresh and engaging new book are a wake-up call for all marketers young and old. Scott's deep and diverse marketing background offers multiple gems for the modern day marketer to win in today's marketplace. I couldn't put the book down and highly recommend it for your reading list."

—**Chris Anderson,** *senior marketing director (large telecom company)*

"A must-read for the twenty-first-century marketer. *The Cuttlefish Marketer* takes the role of data in marketing head on. Most importantly, it calls for marketers to be actively involved and responsible for how data is used. A thoughtful review of how data and marketing are irrevocably linked."

—**Denise Leo,** *vice president, global marketing (large global software company)*

"Our world is being dramatically transformed and turned on its head by powerful forces such as social networks, cloud computing, and big data. The marketing profession is no exception. *The Cuttlefish Marketer* by Scott East and Ivan Aguilar offers a smart, insightful, and compelling perspective on what it will take for a marketing leader to thrive in this brave new world."

—**Fabrice Martin,** *vice president, product management (software company)*

"This is a must-read book for all marketers who started their careers in the B.I. (before Internet) era and for those caught up in the clutter of digital. As relationships between brands and customers evolve, the skills listed in this book will help marketers stay sharp and relevant."

—**Genevieve Yeep,** *CMO, SendForensics*

"Scott is a true modern marketer with a depth of experience harnessing digital data who has successfully facilitated insights for FORTUNE 100 CMOs that have positively impacted their brands. This book does a wonderful job illustrating simple, proven, and effective ways to transform any marketing department into a robust, insightful team."

—**John Foligno,** *CEO, Cubism Group*

"The traits required to be a successful marketer are perfectly encapsulated in this book. As Scott and Ivan point out, no longer can marketers passively adapt to our environments, but instead, like the cuttlefish we must be agile, smart, fast, receptive, and savvy."

—**Kevin Day,** *digital marketer (large wireless company)*

"The world doesn't need another book on marketing. Unless of course, it's Scott East's book that asks you to think and act like a cuttlefish. Scott's reminded me that in over twenty-five years of marketing my best teams have, in fact, acted like cuttlefish. A unique way to think about marketing more quickly in an ever-changing world."

—**Mark Pilipczuk,** *CMO, 25+ year senior marketing executive*

"*The Cuttlefish Marketer* should be an essential read for any marketer. Through Scott's diverse experience and proven success as a marketing leader, he provides an insightful and entertaining view of the essential traits of modern marketers. Whether you're new to the marketing arena or a seasoned vet, the concepts in this book will provide you the tools necessary to be an A+ marketer in the modern age."

—**Monte Beck,** *CMO, 20+ year senior marketing executive*

"Scott possesses unique perspective and marketing expertise based on an eclectic career holding leadership roles as a client, agency, and publisher. It is these perspectives that have enabled Scott to identify key traits that have proven successful as traditional marketing has been disrupted by digital, data, and the emergence of marketing technology. *The Cuttlefish Marketer* is a must-read for those seeking to continually adapt in the ever-evolving world of marketing in the twenty-first century."

—**Stephen Chiles,** *vice president, marketing, 25+ year senior digital marketing executive*

"*The Cuttlefish Marketer* shares essential wisdom to the modern, data-driven marketer who is always pushing the edge of competitiveness by constantly shaping the way to market to the always evolving needs of the consumer. Ivan Aguilar and Scott East share invaluable stories that every digital marketer must take to heart as they go on the daily fight to stay ahead of their competitors—social media and analytics are the new black for twenty-first-century marketers."

—**Arturo Oliver,** *20+ year marketing and technology strategist*

"Without a doubt *The Cuttlefish Marketer* is a book that cannot be missed in any company or marketing department. Despite the fact that marketing is a complex issue or subject, both because of the diversity of means, forms, and types to do it as well as the constant changes and market demands, Ivan and Scott use examples and a simple captivating language that wraps you and helps you understand what marketing is all about and how you can successfully face the constant changes and demands on any type of market in this globalized world."

—**Carlos Avendano,** *general counsel, 20+ year global insurance company executive*

"*The Cuttlefish Marketer* makes us aware that technology and the use of data is the key in understanding our marketing space, audience, and client. In their book, Ivan and Scott list the traits that are essential in a team that can be considered in the forefront of marketing."

—**Rene Mena Seifert,** *CEO, Idesaa, 30+ year executive coach and education programs entrepreneur*

"It is refreshing to find a book like *The Cuttlefish Marketer* among the ocean of new books coming out all the time. This book provides a practical approach to building your marketing team and helped me realize the importance of data analysis in the success of a marketing campaign. I'm fascinated with the comparison between the reactive chameleon and the proactive cuttlefish."

—**Carlos Villareal,** *CEO, MEXI, 20+ year financial services executive*

"Marketers in today's digital world need more customized and sophisticated strategies and approaches. The cuttlefish's tailor-made camouflage ability, adaptability, and agility should be equipped by marketers. I strongly recommend that marketers and CMOs read this book. It's inspiring and very practical."

—**Frida Hong,** *global marketing executive (large technology company)*

The

CUTTLEFISH

MARKETER

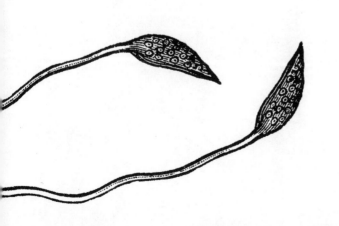

The

CUTTLEFISH

MARKETER

THE FIVE ESSENTIAL TRAITS

OF A MODERN MARKETER

SCOTT EAST &

IVAN AGUILAR

Published by Advantage, Charleston, South Carolina.
Member of Advantage Media Group.

ADVANTAGE is a registered trademark, and the Advantage colophon is a trademark of Advantage Media Group, Inc.

Printed in the United States of America.

ISBN: 978-1-59932-440-1
LCCN: 2016962863

Cover design by George Stevens.
Billy Beane photo courtesy user Muboshgu, licensed under the Creative Commons Attribution 2.0 Generic license.

This publication is designed to provide accurate and authoritative information in regard to the subject matter covered. It is sold with the understanding that the publisher is not engaged in rendering legal, accounting, or other professional services. If legal advice or other expert assistance is required, the services of a competent professional person should be sought.

Advantage Media Group is proud to be a part of the Tree Neutral® program. Tree Neutral offsets the number of trees consumed in the production and printing of this book by taking proactive steps such as planting trees in direct proportion to the number of trees used to print books. To learn more about Tree Neutral, please visit **www.treeneutral.com.**

Advantage Media Group is a publisher of business, self-improvement, and professional development books. We help entrepreneurs, business leaders, and professionals share their Stories, Passion, and Knowledge to help others Learn & Grow. Do you have a manuscript or book idea that you would like us to consider for publishing? Please visit **advantagefamily.com** or call **1.866.775.1696.**

I dedicate this book to my wife, Adriana, for giving me the opportunity to share my life with her, for supporting me through the roads of entrepreneurship, for keeping me company during late-night working hours, for giving me the pride of being a dad, and for all those details that make my life whole. Thank you!

—Ivan Aguilar

This book is dedicated to my incredibly supportive wife, Holley, as well as my entrepreneurial kids, Piper and Ryan. It's also dedicated to my parents who have always supported me, along with my brothers Rick and David; sister Angela; and in-laws, Jan, Jean and Chris Anstatt. Last—but never least—to God, who put together an amazing life and business journey for me.

—Scott East

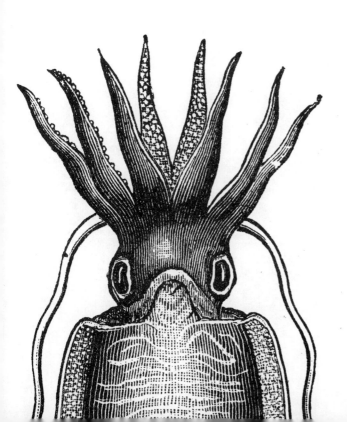

TABLE OF CONTENTS

THE TWENTY-FIRST-CENTURY MARKETER
Chameleons—or Cuttlefish?

TRAIT #1: BE AGILE
*Run Your Marketing Department as a
Hypergrowth Business*

TRAIT #2: DIRECT YOUR TECHNOLOGY
Understand the Important Role Tech Plays in Marketing

TRAIT #3: ACTIVATE DATA
*Embrace Transparency and Accountability
in Order to Learn and Move Fast*

TRAIT #4: DON'T OUTSOURCE YOUR LEADERSHIP
Be an Active Player in Your Own Success

TRAIT #5: BUILD A DIFFERENT KIND OF TEAM
Bring New Skill Sets to the Table

THE FOCUSED, MODERN, MARKETING EXECUTIVE

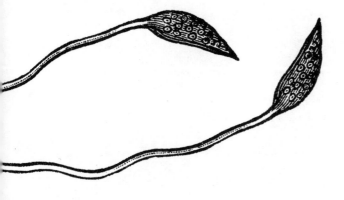

ACKNOWLEDGMENTS

This book became a reality thanks to the support and help of many individuals. I would like to extend my gratitude to all of you for your support not only for this book but also in my journey as an entrepreneur. This journey started many years ago, and it would not be the same if I had not run into a special person, a true leader who has always aimed to be the best. Scott East, thank you for giving me the opportunity to row the boat together, for having the initiative to start this book, and most importantly, for having the endurance to see it through. I would like to express my gratitude to my family for their encouragement and patience toward me, with special mention to my wife, Adriana, who always pushes me to be a better person, and to my children, Ivan, Fernando, Romina, and Melissa, who serve as my drive and inspiration. Thanks to my colleagues in MSIGHTS, past and present; the daily conversations, the challenges we face together, your cleverness, the simplicity, and your optimism make it very easy to spend long hours at the office. Finally, thanks to God for letting me open the doors that have taken me to this day.

—Ivan Aguilar

Marketing was never my path coming out of Syracuse University. I graduated with a political science degree, but after working on an unsuccessful 1992 presidential campaign, I had to find a job. I sent out a ton of resumes to investment banking and management consulting companies, and one went to Dally, a small ad agency in Ft. Worth, TX. It was at Dally where Susan Goiser, Lynda Gearheart, and Scott Dally gave me a chance, and I am forever grateful for it.

Their vote of confidence in me put in motion a very fulfilling career in marketing, advertising, and later technology. And this is where I need to thank former client Ted Moon at Nextel, who gave me a four-month reporting project that evolved into me starting MSIGHTS. But MSIGHTS would never have been MSIGHTS without co-founders Fabrice Martin (my MBA classmate at George-town University) and Ivan Aguilar.

As I think back on these last ten years, I specifically thank Ivan Aguilar, who has continued to be that business partner every entrepreneur wants and needs. Rarely does a day go by—including weekends—when we are not "talking" in some way, whether by phone, chat, or random email thought. To say thanks for the partner-ship is just not enough. I also want to thank my work colleagues Jim Groo, Andres Aguirre, and Christina Woods who helped proof, give feedback, and brainstorm, along with my Entrepreneurs' Organiza-tion Penicillin Forum in Charlotte.

This book has been a two-year journey. Thanks to my executive coach David Sobel who held me accountable to finish the project, to the team at Advantage Media Group, and last but not least, to my writer Ellyn Sanna. Cuttlefish started as a brief metaphor tucked in a random chapter, but then it took on a life of its own. Ellyn, thanks for bringing to life the ideas and for going above and beyond in building the book's narrative.

To my fellow Cuttlefish Marketers, it's always a lot more fun being the predator than the prey. Ivan and I hope you walk away with a few new ideas from reading this book. The marketing ocean is competitive. Stay agile. But don't stand—or swim—still.

—Scott East

For more information about being a Cuttlefish Marketer, visit www.cuttlefishmarketer.com. We'd love to hear your thoughts, too.

Scott East: scott@cuttlefishmarketer.com

Ivan Aguilar: ivan@cuttlefishmarketer.com

INTRODUCTION

Digital data and media have transformed the marketing world. We all know that. Those of us who make our living as marketers find ourselves in a very different reality from the one we knew even ten years ago.

I spent the first part of my career working in the old marketing world—the world where the Internet was only just beginning to be a marketing channel—but in 2004 I created my own company, MSIGHTS, Inc. I sensed that twenty-first-century marketing was becoming a new sort of creature that would need a steady stream of data to feed it.

My twenty-plus years of experience have made one thing clear: today's marketing executives require a different set of skills and strategies from those they once needed to be successful. If marketing departments are going to thrive over the next ten years, they can't keep doing what they've always done. They must radically transform themselves to keep pace with the changes around them.

Data and digital marketing will facilitate this, but I don't want you to think that they're the focus of this book. The real transformation focuses on these five essential traits:

o   agility

o   marketing-directed technology

o   use of data to create transparency, accountability, and fast learning

o   active involvement rather than outsourcing

o   a team with varied skill sets

We'll discuss each of these in the chapters that follow. Together, these traits will transform how you function. Digital data such as social media, search, content, and mobile will be helpful along the way, but it's these five traits that are the critical tools you should have to take advantage of the unbelievably fast current of the modern marketing world.

I've been in the marketing world a long time now. My background includes marketing executive roles as a client (with GTE/Verizon), as an agency partner (at DDB and Mullen), and at a media company (with AOL). What I have experienced and seen in the past five years at MSIGHTS, though, is completely different from what I experienced in the prior years. I had to learn a lot the hard way, through experience and plenty of mistakes.

Now I, alongside my co-author and MSIGHTS co-founder Ivan Aguilar, want to share what we have learned to help ensure *you* have maximum success as a modern marketing leader. We'll tell you how to transform yourself into an entirely different kind of marketing animal, which we call a cuttlefish marketer.

—Scott East

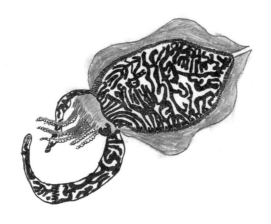

CHAPTER 1

THE TWENTY-FIRST-CENTURY MARKETER

CHAMELEONS—OR CUTTLEFISH?

Chameleons are strange little lizards that can instantly switch their skin color in response to their surroundings. It's a quality that's similar to the swift adaptability required in modern marketing. Those of us who are marketers in today's world must be equally hypersensitive to the slightest changes in our markets, and that sensitivity must then trigger nearly instantaneous strategy adaptation.

Today's business world celebrates teams that can mimic chameleons and adapt their tactics or strategies. In my opinion, though, the chameleon metaphor is limited when it comes to marketing. Chameleons aren't actually all that intelligent, and their responses to their environments are fairly predictable. They change colors, yeah, but that's about it. Color change expresses their emotional states, helps them adjust to temperature variations in their environment, and reactively prevents predators from seeing them. But chameleons don't use their unique abilities to proactively go on the offensive.[1] They're pretty passive little guys. Basically, they just hang out in trees, hoping no one will notice them while they wait for food to come along. That's really not a good strategy to imitate if you want to be successful in today's competitive marketing arena.

Chameleon   Cuttlefish

Cuttlefish, on the other hand, are intelligent and proactive predators, and they have camouflage abilities that make a chameleon's look like a child's trick. Cuttlefish adopt a more personalized, adapted, and targeted approach by using data from the environment to adapt their appearance. A cuttlefish is a kind of mollusk, and you probably don't connect smarts with mollusks, but we're not talking here about your average clam or oyster. Scientists believe that these odd relatives of octopus and squids have highly evolved brains that allow them to search out and capture their prey, which they do at top speed, using a form of jet propulsion to power through the water. Best of all, their ability to manipulate their appearance isn't a question of merely changing skin color the way a chameleon does. Instead, according to

Roger Hanlon, senior scientist at the Marine Biological Laboratory at Woods Hole, Massachusetts, "Each animal adopts a tailor-made camouflage pattern for the particular microhabitat that it settles in. An animal that settles in sand will appear one way, and ten feet away, where it's all algae, another will be camouflaged differently."[2]

As marketers in today's digital world, we require something more sophisticated than a chameleon's camouflage abilities. Unlike chameleons, we *want* to be noticed, and we need a far more can-do, take-charge approach than just hiding out and hoping customers will stumble onto us. Instead, we constantly and actively pursue our customers, using one strategy in one situation, adapting and fine-tuning that for a shift in the market, and then coming up with completely different tactics and methods for yet another set of circumstances. And we have to do it all at blinding speeds. We must have the cuttlefish's level of adaptability, not a chameleon's.

But that's enough for now about little critters out there in the natural world. Let me give you a couple of examples that will show you how the chameleon-versus-cuttlefish analogy makes sense of the marketing arenas of yesterday and today.

THE MARLBORO MAN VERSUS THE OLD SPICE GUY

Remember the Marlboro Man? Lean-hipped, narrow-eyed, quiet, the perfect picture of rugged masculinity. Blue skies, mountain ranges, fence posts, and an occasional horse were his only backgrounds. Like a chameleon perched on its branch, the Marlboro Man didn't really do much. He just hung out, smoking a cigarette, his cowboy hat tipped over his face. Once upon a time, his static, silent image was the epitome of successful marketing.

According to *Advertising Age,* the Marlboro Man was the most powerful brand image of the twentieth century.[3] His decades-long advertising reign, from 1954 to 1999, successfully changed Marlboro cigarettes from a feminine brand that was "Mild as May" into the ultimate masculine trademark and the best-selling cigarette in the world.

The Marlboro Man was a brilliant piece of marketing that, like a chameleon, easily adapted to a range of environments. Leo Burnett Worldwide, the advertising agency who brought him to life, used every media channel available to them at the time to tell the Marlboro Man story. Each magazine image and billboard (portraying macho strength and wide-open spaces), each word of ad copy ("the man-size flavor of honest tobacco"), the jingle (which sounded like the opening to the most heart-stirring Western movie ever), every piece of branded merchandise, and even the packaging, all reinforced the message that Marlboro cigarettes represented the all-American man: strong, independent, competent, courageous, and close to the earth. In each media setting, he remained essentially the same, and if you notice, the man rarely moved. With his arm hooked over a fence post, his hand resting on his bent knee, or his fingers cupped around a cigarette, he was basically the manliest chameleon you ever saw hanging out in the trees. That macho lure was his single strategy.

Today the Marlboro Man is no longer a hero. Smoking has proved to be not very manly (given the fact that it can kill you), but even if he were selling a far more innocuous product—say, Viagra or pickup trucks—his silence would be lost in the constant racket and movement of twenty-first-century media. Today's marketing isn't based on the long-term campaign focused on a single unchanging message that adapts only to the point where it can work on TV as well as in a magazine ad. The Marlboro Man is, figuratively, dead. A new guy has taken his place as the epitome of successful marketing.

As did Marlboro cigarettes, Old Spice cologne once epitomized traditional masculinity. It had a seventy-year heritage of manliness, but the old brand image wasn't working in the twenty-first century. Then, during the Super Bowl, the cologne company introduced the Old Spice Guy, "the man your man could smell like," and everything changed.

The ad not only played during the Super Bowl; it also amassed 220,000 YouTube views in just a few hours after the game, and then it went viral, gaining about 100,000 new views every few hours. A social media campaign came next, with personalized video responses to questions asked by fans on Twitter and YouTube. The fast-paced, interactive videos included the Old Spice Guy beating a piñata with a big fish, helping a guy propose to his girlfriend, and engaging in an energetic flirtation with the actress Alyssa Milano. Forty-eight hours into the social media outreach, Old Spice had nearly eleven million video views. It had also gained about 29,000 new Facebook followers and 58,000 Twitter followers.

While the Marlboro Man never did much of anything except occasionally ride a horse and hang out on a fence, the Old Spice Guy was in your face and laugh-out-loud silly. If the Marlboro Man had been a passive, chameleon-like strategy, the Old Spice Guy was definitely a cuttlefish approach to marketing: proactive, fast, and really, really smart. Old Spice used him to go hand-to-hand in a constantly moving, light-on-its-feet marketing battle. And they kept it going tirelessly.

The Old Spice Guy next went "mano a mano en el baño" against supermodel Fabio, with both men submitting responses to the same posts on Twitter, Facebook, and YouTube, while fans voted in real time for their favorites. The Old Spice Guy's personal messages were scripted and filmed and lasted ten to fifteen minutes each. More than

186 short videos went out into the world in the space of forty-eight hours. Together, Fabio and Old Spice Guy got more than sixty-five million views.

Ultimately, Twitter followers of Old Spice increased by 2,700 percent, while Facebook fans rose from 500,000 to 800,000, and subscribers to the brand's YouTube channel more than doubled, from 65,000 to 150,000. Even more important, sales went up by 125 percent, and Old Spice became the number-one brand of men's body wash in the United States.

IMPACT OF OLD SPICE VIRAL CAMPAIGN

	Before Super Bowl Commercial	After Super Bowl Commercial	Change
Facebook fans	500,000	800,000	+300,000
YouTube subscribers	65,000	150,000	+85,000

→ Sales Increase by 125%   → #1 body wash in the United States

Clearly, the Old Spice Guy was a brilliant piece of marketing, but it was the fans that drove Old Spice's success. Instead of a bunch of ad agency execs and creatives making consistent content for a static, long-term image such as the Marlboro Man, now the fans themselves pushed the content back and forth in a fast-paced, real-time dance that was so responsive, so light on its feet, that it could switch directions nearly instantly. Jason Bagley, creative director at Wieden+Kennedy, the advertising agency responsible for the Old Spice Guy, told *Inc.*, "The key is interacting with consumers and building a relationship that's not just putting out a TV spot every once in a while and hoping that works."[4] This kind of marketing creates an ongoing relationship with an audience that is deeply engaged in real-time conversations.

"What made the Response Campaign a success was the fact that it felt like a campaign for everyone. It wasn't an exclusive idea but a wholly inclusive one. It was about moving from mass media TV, print and digital to engagement—still targeting the same audience, but deepening the communication and similarly the relationship."

—Britton Taylor, planner, Wieden+Kennedy[5]

While twentieth-century marketing focused on emotional responses to create a fixed mind-set, the twenty-first century's marketing culture is both more data driven and more fluid. It embraces the power of technology to create a constantly changing image of the world. As a result, when it comes to the purchases buyers make, salespeople are no longer the key sources of information. Instead, countless social media and content-focused outlets combine to give consumers the information they use to make buying decisions.

The digital world has changed our reality. Effective marketing departments now depend on a constant flow of well-organized digital information. Old Spice, for example, needed a multitude of social comments rapidly compiled and assessed for creative potential. The more than a billion unpaid, earned media impressions were also a major metric that had to be gathered and understood. The huge amount of constantly changing data had to be analyzed and delivered in a meaningful way to the marketing department. Data is essential to the cuttlefish marketer.

MARKETING DATA

Research from 360i found that consumers spend almost $300,000 a minute shopping online; brands are liked 350,000 times per minute on Facebook; and Twitter users send more than 600,000 tweets per hour.[6] The magnitude and specificity of this information has given rise to an entire industry that focuses on marketing data.

This data offers not only statistical analysis but also behavioral data and social media analysis that marketing and sales departments can use to discover answers to specific questions. Marketing departments can now study multiple, co-occurring buyer behaviors based on past purchases to predict future buying behaviors. Social monitoring analytics can be applied to the same information that buyers are exposed to through blogs and social media. Marketing teams have access to countless meaningful insights into who is talking about their products, what they are saying, and what and who is influencing them.

This customer data is collected via billions of connected devices, including smartphones, PCs, RFID sensors, beacons, gaming devices, and now our automobiles. The data is not only immense in volume but also moves at a breakneck speed. If marketing departments can't respond equally fast, the information will be useless because it's already out of date.

Today marketing data offers insights into which content is the most effective at each stage of a sales cycle. It provides the foundation for strategies for increasing conversion rates, prospect engagement, and revenue, and it allows companies to optimize their pricing strategies. Most of all, though, it gives marketing departments what they require to create the new form of customer engagement and fast-on-its-feet responses that the Old Spice Guy exemplifies. (We'll talk a lot more about data in chapter 4.)

SOME EXAMPLES OF THE WAYS IN WHICH MARKETING DATA IS CHANGING THE WAY COMPANIES DO BUSINESS

○ Red Roof Inn utilizes weather information to target stranded airport passengers, using search advertising, mobile communications, and other digital methods to drive bookings with personalized messages like "Stranded at Dulles? Check out Red Roof Inn."[7]

○ Wal-Mart increased online sales by 15 percent (millions of dollars) by using semantic search algorithms to understand what someone is searching for. It culls through millions of tweets, Facebook messages, blog postings, YouTube videos, and more to detect purchase intent and drive e-commerce.[8]

○ Capital One analyzes the demographic data and spending habits of customers to determine the most optimal times to present various offers to clients. This increases the conversion rates of their offers, while at the same time gaining more leads from their marketing budget.[9]

NO LONGER THE KIDS' TABLE

Back in the mid to late nineties was when the company where I worked first ventured into digital marketing. At that point in time, we were creating banner campaigns on portals (remember those?). The Internet was accessed through dial-up modems, so everything was so much slower and clunkier. Still, some of us could see how much marketing potential there was in the digital world. But we had a long way to go.

Remember when you were young and you had to eat at the kids' table every Thanksgiving at Grandma's house? Well, back in the

1990s, it felt as if all the big branding took place at the adults' table in the dining room, with television in the chair at the head; print, radio, and outdoor advertising seated around the table; and direct mail in the chair way down at the foot. And digital marketing? Well, it was seated at a folding card table somewhere out in the living room, away from the grown-ups.

No one wants to sit at the kids' table forever. The one thing that we digital marketers had going for us was data. So, early on, we embraced that as a way to fight for a seat at the big table. Eventually, digital marketing gained momentum. It not only got its seat at the table but also shoved everyone else there to the side. Now, we're the ones sitting at the head of the table.

> *"I grew up hearing grown-ups who said, 'It can't be done. Don't waste your time. Stick to what works.' So I got bored with grown-ups. My cousins and I figured out new things all the time. Some of them worked, some of them didn't. Some of them got us in trouble, some of them got us the sixth-grade version of praise and glory. Either way, it was interesting. And in the end, I learned something important—if you try what's never been done, sometimes it works. It doesn't have to work all the time. The smallest nudge can trigger an avalanche. And then from there, things start to gain momentum. The people who told you it couldn't be done find themselves living in a whole new reality."*
>
> —Larry Paige, inventor[10]

CUTTLEFISH MARKETING TRAITS

The flood of digital data drove the shift in marketing that we're still seeing today. It's what created the environment where fast, adaptable cuttlefish marketers thrive. Digital marketing is an example—as social media is—of one jet stream that keeps the speed accelerating, and it's organically integrated with digital data, allowing marketing to be instantly responsive to customers in a way that it never was able to be before.

The Old Spice Guy demonstrates perfectly the way marketing can successfully ride the combined current of the five cuttlefish traits we'll be discussing in this book. The campaign's success wouldn't have been possible without a marketing director who (1) both understood and managed how the information technology (IT) pieces fit together, (2) was able to use data to learn fast and go with whatever worked, and (3) didn't rely exclusively on outside partners such as agencies to create success. All that was possible because (4) the Old Spice Guy was created and supported by an entirely different kind of marketing team, one that brought a wide range of practical skill sets that made all the moving parts possible. Together, those four characteristics—marketing-directed technology; the use of data to create transparency, accountability, and fast learning; active involvement rather than outsourcing; and a team with varied skill sets—supported and empowered the first essential trait: cuttlefish agility.

"The world is being reshaped by the convergence of social, mobile, cloud, big data, community and other powerful forces. The combination of these technologies unlocks an incredible opportunity to connect everything together in a new way."

—Marc Benioff, Chairman and CEO, Salesforce[11]

15

KEY POINTS TO REMEMBER

→ Today's marketing culture is radically different from what it was even ten years ago.

→ Modern marketing is data driven.

→ The power of technology allows marketers to use data to drive marketing.

→ Modern marketing has to be fast, responsive, and agile.

CHAPTER 2

TRAIT #1: BE AGILE

RUN YOUR MARKETING DEPARTMENT AS A HYPERGROWTH BUSINESS

Cuttlefish demonstrate an amazing ability to adapt quickly and creatively to the demands of their environment. Scientists compare these creatures' phenomenally fast skin changes to the technology that creates color on high-definition television, combining the primary colors to form complex shades and shifting patterns. But cuttlefish's abilities don't stop there. Not only can they change colors in a far more sophisticated way than chameleons do but they're also shape-shifters. They can use their muscles to actually change the texture and contours of their skin, making themselves look like seaweed, rocks, or even fishnets.[12] These incredibly prompt responses to their environment apparently involve intelligence and choice, according to researchers who have found that cuttlefish use differing skin changes for communication, for pursuing prey in different environments, and for finding mates.[13]

The cuttlefish's swift adaptability isn't some nice-to-have skill it has on the side. It has integrated an immediate reaction to its environment into everything it does. Its responsive speed is what makes it such an agile predator of the sea. In a similar way, today's marketing department can't pull adaptability out from its back pocket as though it were a pocketknife that might come in useful now and then. Instead, rapid responsiveness has to be inherent in marketing's overall function. It's not an occasional option to implement; it's the essential skill that pulls everything together. It's what makes the marketing department's function integral with the entire life force of a hypergrowth business.

Cuttlefish marketers are agile. They run their marketing departments as though they are hypergrowth businesses.

"Marketing agility in action requires the bridging of gaps in data, knowledge, process, technology, and people. A best-in-class Marketing Operations function operates like a true Chief of Staff to enable the CMO and marketing to lead the company through business intelligence, accountability, and building business cases. An agile marketing group can lead the company in spurring change, seizing opportunities, and doing the whole job."

—Gary Katz, Chairman of Marketing Operations Partners[14]

HYPERGROWTH BUSINESS QUALITIES

Successful businesses today have to be agile. They can't rest on their laurels, remaining the same from year to year. As any good cuttlefish is, they also have to be constantly responsive to their environment and willing to constantly transform themselves in response to circumstances that continuously change.

Dyson Ltd. is a good example of a business whose growth has depended on its agile responsiveness to customer demand. "We're only as good as our latest product," James Dyson said recently.[15] He has built his vacuum cleaner company around innovations that consumers can see and experience for themselves. Dyson's words are not just a marketing slogan; they're the core of his business operation.

If Dyson had followed conventional wisdom when he was starting out, he would have entered the market with products that were cheaper than those of Hoover, the entrenched market leader. Instead, Dyson's initial vacuum cleaners cost two or three times more than Hoover's, but they promised consumers improved efficiency as a result of Dyson's ingenuity and innovation.

Dyson's entire business philosophy centers on his innovation. The business he built consistently thinks outside the box, adapts quickly in response to customer reactions, and never allows a sense of status quo to take hold of its company culture. In 2012, not quite twenty years after James Dyson founded his company, his vacuum cleaners overtook Hoover, their hundred-year-old competitor, and became the top-selling upright vacuum cleaner in the United States. Dyson's innovation disrupted the entire market and created a new reality for vacuum cleaners. Today the company is a hypergrowth business that continues to reinvent its products again and again.

Dyson's disruptive ingenuity isn't limited to its products. The company also has an innovative way of looking at how a business should function. Dyson doesn't employ technicians but instead asks that its engineers and scientists actually go out and build prototypes based on their own ideas. Instead of seeing research and development, production, marketing, and management as separately functioning departments, the company integrates them so that they can work together to respond quickly and powerfully to consumers. Dyson's marketing strategy and its overall business strategy are nearly identical.

James Dyson firmly believes that a company's profits should be invested back into research and development rather than into marketing that continues to sell an ordinary product purely on the strength of the way it's advertised. Instead of spending money on a new advertising campaign to encourage customers to buy a product that may not actually meet their needs, Dyson aims to change and adapt his products in revolutionary ways so they work better. To achieve this, his company invests in customer data as well as research, testing, and development to discover exactly how to meet consumer demands.

In the past, even before the big data revolution took hold, the company introduced new products based on questionnaires sent out to existing customers. In one instance, nearly eighty thousand people responded, letting the company have information about their lifestyles, their cleaning needs, their floor surfaces, their environmental concerns, and both their satisfaction and frustration with existing Dyson models. Then, as new prototypes were developed in response to all this feedback, the company tried them out with focus groups that were carefully selected to be representative of the overall population.[16] This range of customer information, combined with research into competitor products, drove the company's next development and marketing strategy, giving Dyson the competitive edge it required to maintain its hypergrowth status.

This concept of swift, data-based responsiveness to customers extends to every part of Dyson, including product design, engineering, patenting, sales, customer care, and after sales. James Dyson emphasizes testing, data analysis, and agile innovation to drive his company's growth.

The modern marketing department must be as agile as a hypergrowth business such as Dyson. Research done at Massachusetts Institute of Technology (MIT) found that agile firms grow revenue 37 percent faster and generate 30 percent higher profits than nonagile companies.[17] Sounds great, but how do we make ourselves agile?

AGILE MARKETING

These days, professionals in the business world talk constantly about agility. Do a Google search for "business agility," and you'll get more than eight million results. We all know that agile is what we want to be, but we don't always know exactly what it is we mean by agility.

We already know *Merriam-Webster's Dictionary's* definition of agility: "able to move quickly, easily, and lightly; able to learn and understand things quickly and easily; the quality of being resourceful and adaptable." But what does moving quickly and easily look like to those of us who are marketing executives? What specific things should we learn quickly and easily? What are we adapting to? How does being resourceful look within the modern marketing world?

The concept of agility is also important to software engineering and to manufacturing, but this isn't always helpful to our understanding as marketers. While the methodologies developed around these kinds of agility create good analogies for marketers, they can't quite be applied literally. The general concept is enough to get us pointed in the right direction, of course, and that's a good start, but we must understand how to specifically apply agility to marketing if we want to become cuttlefish marketers.

So first, let's talk about manufacturing agility a little more. The software engineer Roger Pressman believes agility consists of

- rapid and adaptive response to change,

- effective communication among all stakeholders,

- drawing the customer onto the team, and

- organizing a team so that it is in control of the work performed.

All of this, according to Pressman, is done to yield rapid, incremental delivery of software—or whatever the product is. The process of agile delivery, he goes on to say,

- is driven by customer descriptions of what is required (scenarios),

- recognizes that plans are short lived,

- develops the product iteratively (rather than with a final version in mind),

- delivers multiple increments toward the final goal, and

- adapts as changes occur.[18]

Pressman's talking specifically about software engineering. From a more generic manufacturing perspective, agility is simply the ability to adjust supply to meet changing demand. The more agile your manufacturing process, the faster you'll be able to do this.

Let's say you're manufacturing blue dresses that take a full month to create, and suddenly your consumers no longer want blue dresses. Now they want red dresses. Since your manufacturing time is a month, it's going to take you a full month to adapt to your market. If, however, you can produce a dress in a day, you can shift your production within twenty-four hours to meet customer demand. This means you're really agile and you'll be able to beat out slower-moving competitors.

The potential implications for marketing are fairly clear. However, marketers don't manufacture anything except, perhaps, ideas. We're not creating software and we're not creating dresses or building widgets. The things we need to learn and adapt to are not quite the same. The entire concept of supply and demand is a lot fuzzier when we're talking about marketing. Our processes are not the same as a manufacturer's or an engineer's.

According to the Chartered Institute of Marketing, "Marketing is the management process responsible for identifying, anticipating, and satisfying customer requirements profitably."[19] When we apply the concept of agility to that definition, it looks like this: "Marketing agility is the speed at which you can adjust your process to identify and deliver customer value—and make more money." Note that marketing agility is *not* the speed at which you execute a campaign. A railroad engine is speedy, but it's not at all agile.

Joel York, CEO and founder of Markodojo, believes your marketing agility equates to "how fast you can change your product, adjust your price, deliver a new promotion or shift your channels to anticipate and satisfy ever changing customer needs."[20] Parallel to Pressman's description of engineering agility, York offers these practices of the agile marketer:

- Measure value through the eyes of the customer. *Customer value is the fundamental axis of alignment for marketing.*

- Minimize waste by reducing uncertainty. *Producing anything that is not valuable to the customer is waste.*

- Maximize flexibility by working incrementally. *Small, incremental adjustments to the marketing mix take less time to complete than large, monolithic adjustments.*

- Foster alignment and collaboration through transparency. *Marketing managers must reach well outside the marketing department to align customers with the company by facilitating marketing activities in sales, engineering, manufacturing, finance, and so on. The more transparent the marketing management process, the more effective the facilitation.*

- Improve iteratively and continuously. *Effective marketing makes money for the company, and this will only happen if marketing builds upon past successes and learns from past mistakes.*[21]

Each of York's agility practices are expressed in the other four traits of my cuttlefish marketer: responsive IT that gives decision makers the ability to access the right information at the right time, accountability and transparency that's based on well-activated data, initiative within professional partnerships, and the flexible management of well-chosen teams.

Ultimately, the critical qualities of an agile marketer can be summed up like this: rapid decision making and execution to drive value. For the cuttlefish marketer, this has to be done within a much larger context than ever before.

THINK BIG

In the twenty-first century, marketing cannot function in a separate silo that's removed from the rest of the business. Today's marketing directors must think big—and they can't rely exclusively on an external agency to do it all for them. (We'll talk about this more in chapter 5.) It is necessary to integrate marketing with the entire business, and marketing directors must run their departments with the same priorities as the CEO of a hypergrowth business such as Dyson.

The Chartered Institute of Marketing's definition of marketing that we mentioned earlier—"Marketing is the management process responsible for identifying, anticipating and satisfying customer requirements profitably"—acknowledges that customers are the focus of marketing, but it indicates at the same time that marketing departments are directly responsible for their companies' profitability, which in turn implies that marketing directors will have to embrace other business operations in order to do this. Evaluation and measurement—data, in other words—underpin all of these, as does the ability to respond quickly and think strategically.

Decades-long advertising campaigns such as the Marlboro Man's can't achieve this. Can you imagine James Dyson ever pinning his company's success to a single, iconic symbol the way Marlboro did? In contrast to Dyson's approach, however, from 2008 to 2013, Hoover consistently used the same marketing slogan, promoting its brand image of unchanging dependability.

Meanwhile, James Dyson insisted he didn't even have a brand. His statement brought him the disapproval of *Forbes* magazine[22] and *Advertising Age*,[23] which both insisted that Dyson had worked hard to market its "no-brand brand." The fact is, however, that Mr. Dyson's brand is his reputation for innovation, and building and maintaining that brand is critical. The company keeps its ingenuity constantly attuned to what will make profits and changes accordingly.

Now let's take a look at a company that couldn't keep up in today's world. In 1976 Kodak was a $30 billion corporation that produced film, a medium consumers used for recording their memories. In the twentieth century, the company's marketing term, "the Kodak moment," was so successful that it entered the common language to describe a personal event that demanded to be recorded for posterity.

Once digitalization came along, people could suddenly store their memories in a new way, but Kodak wasn't worried. At the time, personal computers' memory was so small that uploading an image from a camera to a computer was a painfully long process. Kodak's executives deceived themselves into thinking that digital cameras were no threat to their business. They didn't realize that their company's sheer size wouldn't protect it. Instead of being nimble and responsive to its market, the company sat there like a beached behemoth, not realizing that the tide was going out around it.

As computer technology improved by leaps and bounds, people stopped buying film and began saving their memories as digital media. Eventually, the smartphone integrated all the technology into a single mobile device. In 1976 Kodak sold 90 percent of the photographic film in the United States and 85 percent of the cameras,[24] but by 2009, one year after Apple launched the iPhone, Kodak was no longer on the Standard & Poor's 500 index. The once-successful corporation had lost millions of dollars and laid off thousands of people, all because it was too slow to change its business model to respond to consumer demands.

Today's marketing departments should think as James Dyson does and not as Kodak did. No longer can we simply keep doing the same things we once did successfully, year after year. To do so is a formula for failure, as Kodak found out too late. Now we must be willing to adapt and change as often as we need to in order to keep pace with the rapidly changing world in which we do business. To do this, we have to keep our eye on the big picture, always remembering that the picture is not a static one; it's always in flux.

To be like Dyson and not like Kodak, we have to be fast and nimble enough to respond to market changes nearly instantly. When I was starting out in the marketing world, back in the early 1990s, moving fast wasn't as important as it is today. Now, it's a necessity.

"Every success story is a tale of constant adaption, revision and change. A company that stands still will soon be forgotten."

—Richard Branson, founder, Virgin[25]

NO MORE DARK-SIDE-OF-THE-MOON MARKETING

Remember the days of the NASA moon launches? As the Apollo rocket ship lifted off from Kennedy Space Center, the entire world watched with excitement. Every word the astronauts communicated to mission control was televised. But the moment came when the Apollo spacecraft went around the moon to the dark side, where no radio communication with Earth was possible. The folks in Houston's mission control, along with the rest of the world, held their breaths, waiting . . . waiting . . . until the ship came around the moon and back into communication. That silent dark-side-of-the-moon experience was a lot like the gap between the beginning of an old-style marketing campaign and the point at which customer response revealed whether it had been successful.

To start with, you had to have a long lead time whenever you created an advertising campaign. The processes involved were all slow: first you had to create a strategy brief, then a creative brief, then creative development, production, and approvals. Every step was slow. TV ads took time to create and distribute; print ads were nearly as time consuming. This meant that your marketing message had to be locked in place weeks before your advertising was printed or broadcast on TV and radio.

With all the busywork you had to wade through before an ad campaign went out into the world, the message itself had to be pretty much set in stone. If you tried to change it midstream, you'd be in big trouble. For good or ill, you were stuck with it. Now you just had to wait to see if it worked.

At NASA, once the spacecraft came back into communication, it would do an enormous data dump into the computers at Houston. The same sort of thing happened as responses came in to a campaign except, unfortunately, they didn't come in all at once the way the Apollo's data had. Instead, marketers had to wait to be able to project a response curve that would allow them to decide whether to continue the campaign or stop it. Like mission control hoping against hope that the Apollo spacecraft would make it around the moon, marketers had to wait and see if their campaigns would pay off. If the campaigns flopped, both time and money would have been wasted.

This slow-moving, dark-side-of-the-moon marketing scenario was where Hoover vacuum cleaners and Marlboro cigarettes thrived, selling year after year with very little change in either the product or the message. The Old Spice Guy would never have survived back then. He couldn't even have existed.

In the 1990s, however, direct-mail campaigns led us away from that dark-side-of-the-moon suspense. A friend of mine, Mark Pilipczuk, who worked in marketing for International Masters Publishers, participated in mailing out recipe cards as a way to build relationships with consumers. IMP's direct-mail response curves and modeling were sophisticated and accurate, and they proved that data-driven feedback was the foundation for an agile, growing business.

Today's technology has allowed the marketing process to become still more effective, sending it into warp drive. There is no dark-side-of-the-moon waiting now. Digital marketing has expanded the efficiency of the 1990s' direct-mail campaigns even further, offering immediate customer data and results feedback that are based on activities such as click history or click stream analysis, so that marketing departments now know, for example, exactly what interests consumers by seeing the pages they visit and in what order. Customer data is so dynamic and such a fast-moving and constantly changing stream that marketing departments have to be incredibly flexible and faster than the wind to keep up.

THINK FAST

Sociologists and economists tell us that today's business world moves faster than ever before. Take one of the world's largest companies in terms of market value, Apple. Every *millisecond* another customer downloads an Apple app; consumers purchase a thousand iPhones, iPads, or Macs every couple of minutes; the company turns over its inventories in just four days; and every four weeks, it launches a new product.[26] Although Apple may be an extreme example, nearly all twenty-first-century businesses feel the pressure to move fast.

This rapid-fire business activity is in response to a world that's equally hyperactive. In today's global world, new products travel far more quickly than ever before. For example, when the spinning mule, which allowed cotton thread to be rapidly wound onto a spindle, was invented in England two hundred and fifty years or so ago, the rest of the world didn't catch on for more than a hundred years. When mobile phones were invented, however, within only thirteen years, the entire world was using them.[27] The speed of communication, e-commerce, and increased media exposure are some of the reasons for this, all of which are the result of the digital world in which we live.

Marketing customization used to be thought of as something that was done in very small-scale scenarios. Today, mass customization has become the norm. As a result, companies can no longer have just the single marketing focus that Marlboro and Hoover had. The Internet's manic speed means that high-velocity, constantly changing marketing is essential. Old-style marketing practices simply can't survive in today's lightning-paced world. If you can't move as nimbly and swiftly as the market does, you'll never keep up.

Marketers don't create software programs or manufacture widgets. What we do produce is content to feed the digital media. Gone are the days when a single image of the Marlboro Man could be plastered on both billboards and magazine pages. Today's media are hungry for a constant diet of fresh, engaging, and ever-evolving innovative content, made up of high-quality information, images, and stories, each targeted to the unique requirements of a particular media format and in many cases very specific audience segments.

Back in the day, a piece of creative content could last for months. Today its life expectancy is measured in hours or even minutes. The average half-life of a link on Facebook, for example, is 3.2 hours, while the total lifespan of a typical tweet is said to be 2.8 hours[28] (although many people believe the lifespan of a tweet is actually closer to twenty minutes[29]). Many factors account for the speed of content turnover, but mostly, I suspect, it's the interaction between new inventions, the human mind, and the consumer's expectation of change.

Think about it. Back in 1946, when one of the earliest electronic digital computers, the ENIAC, was built, it cost $400,000, weighed thirty tons, and filled a 1,500-square-foot room. Its forty cabinets, each of them nine feet high, were packed with 18,000 vacuum tubes, 10,000 capacitors, 6,000 switches, and 1,500 relays.[30] Just thirty-three years later, the Apple II, an affordable computer that fit on a desktop, was released. Less than three decades after that, the first MacBook was released with 667 MHz, and only a decade later, the iPhone came out with more than twice that power. It also had more computing power than NASA did when it sent astronauts to the moon in 1969. In fact, the iPhone 6 can perform instructions 120,000,000 times faster than the best Apollo-era computers.[31] Now think about the amount of information that's available on the Internet—compared to the old days, when we had to get information and entertainment from printed media—and consider that the information on the Web is expected to increase by 500 percent by 2021.[32] Clearly, the media world is whizzing by at faster and faster speeds.

While we focus on staying ahead, we have to do a tremendous amount of work just to keep up. With so much fleet-footed change in the world, combined with a market attention span that's getting shorter and shorter, it becomes all the more important that businesses cultivate versatility, flexibility, and agility. They can't get attached to the status quo any more than James Dyson could afford to devote himself and his

company to his original vacuum cleaner model. If he hadn't been able to respond swiftly and agilely to market demands, he would never have been able to take over the market. Hyper-growth businesses such as his have to be able to think and move fast and so do today's marketing departments.

Being agile requires speed, but speed alone won't be enough. Speed is good but not if it means you're simply doing the same things over and over, faster and faster. The fastest cuttlefish in the sea may not be the most successful if it can't catch its prey once it's caught up with it. Instead, the cuttlefish's speed is engaged with its environment to sense and respond to stimuli fast enough to drive the most appropriate result for the environment's demands. The cuttlefish marketer wants to be fast in a similar way, quickly responsive to changes in the market.

> *"Marketing agility isn't just about doing things faster. It's about being adaptable to abrupt shifts in customer needs and industry developments. In most cases, dialing up your nimbleness requires more than a team tune-up—usually, it requires nothing short of a transformation."*
>
> —Shelly Lucas, Content Marketing Director, Dun & Bradstreet[33]

THE CONSUMER'S IN THE DRIVER'S SEAT

When I started my career in the early 1990s, people talked about marketing in terms of either the agency side or the client side, as though they existed on opposite sides of a continental divide. If you crossed over from the agency side to the client side, you felt as though you had to journey a vast distance, necessitating an enormous shift in your perspective. If I were working on the agency side, I focused on coming up with strategic communication ideas for advertising campaigns, but I had little understanding of the business as a whole. Meanwhile, if I worked on the client side, marketing communications was only a small part of what I did. I also had a lot of other responsibilities in bringing a campaign to launch such as product management coordination, pricing, legal, regulatory, and sales channels.

Things were starting to change in the 1980s and 1990s, but in the good old days of advertising, back in the 1960s and 1970s, when some ad people were much closer to the stereotypes represented by Don Draper of *Mad Men*, a business's choice of an advertising campaign was generally based on personal preference (perhaps with some research backing up the idea). If a marketing director liked an agency's idea, the company generally went with it. Creativity was rewarded, sometimes with actual awards, but it was rarely measured or analyzed, and a lot of ego stroking went on at the same time that had nothing to do with what customers actually liked or wanted. Results weren't celebrated as much as creative ideas were.

Today, thanks to the digital revolution, reading the market is a fundamental skill that all successful marketing directors should have. This requires many of the same qualities that Dyson has demonstrated: a rigorous analysis of consumers' requirements and characteristics, meticulous mapping of the competitive landscape, and the ability to precisely define what makes your own company different from all others, uniquely able to satisfy customers. Whatever marketing strategy you use, the customer is always in the driver's seat.

> *"The ability to adapt quickly to changes in consumer behaviour—such as the move towards shopping across discounters and traditional supermarkets, or the growth of online shopping and the rise of social media—is vital as it requires brands to rethink how they present themselves to the world."*
>
> —Dom Dwight, Marketing Director, Yorkshire Tea (Taylors of Harrogate)[34]

THE MARKETING BATTLEFIELD

Prior to the twentieth century, warfare was a very different thing from what it is today. Back then, generals could draw diagrams of their campaigns on maps. Soldiers marched out to battle in orderly formation. Sometimes the campaign was a success; sometimes it was a horrifying disaster. There was no way to know for sure what would happen until you fought the battle. Modern technology has revolutionized warfare, just as it has so much of human life. Today's battles are usually small and fast. Guerilla warfare has taken the place of enormous, regimented battle plans. The enemy won't stand still, waiting for an attack, and the slow-moving cavalry of past centuries wouldn't have a chance in today's world.

The transformation of the marketing world is similar. In the old days, an advertising agency developed a campaign through a series of orderly steps. First, account execs at the agency came up with a strategy brief, which they presented to the rest of the agency, including the creative team, for feedback. Once it had been fine-tuned, the next step was to show it to the client. The client gave feedback, the agency came back with new or adapted ideas, the client gave more feedback, and finally, everyone agreed on creative execution. The agency then started executing ideas across the individual marketing channels (TV, radio, print, direct mail, and digital). Finally, it was time to go back and meet again with the client. The client looked at all the pieces of the media plan and approved or disapproved them. A lot of revisions usually came next until all the creative pieces were at last in place to be launched. The campaign ran—it got store traffic, for example—and eventually, the agency and client obtained feedback.

That style of marketing was a lot like a heavy, cumbersome, battle machine, lumbering out onto the field. Millions of dollars would have been pumped into the thing, and no one had any real idea if it would work or not.

Everything's different now. Today, anything you map out ahead of time has to be easily changed and adapted; your plans have to be fluid and flexible. Keep in mind that it's not just a matter of responding quickly to changes in the marketplace; you're also coming up against competitors who are doing the same thing. Your war isn't being fought on one front or even two. Instead, countless players are all interacting at once. Who knows what could happen in the world between the time you have an idea and the time you execute it? The world economy could have plunged into a recession or been rocked by something like Brexit (the United Kingdom's vote to leave the EU); new competitors might have entered your marketplace; your competitors' advertising may make yours obsolete.

If you're not agile and fast on your feet, you won't be able to respond to whatever happens. You'll be standing there in formation, all your guns pointing at absolutely nothing, while the rest of the world has taken the battle somewhere else entirely. Instead of that clumsy, slow-moving regiment, you need marketing that's a lot more like a Navy SEAL team whose members are skilled individuals, agile and adaptable. They can take fast action in a wide variety of ways, functioning as a Dyson does rather than as a Hoover does. (We'll be talking more about how to build your team in chapter 6.)

> *"Do you see an acorn and think 'tree' or do you see an acorn and think 'squirrel'? You need to think squirrel these days... if you aren't nimble and able to see the world through the eyes of different customers, the world will quickly pass you by."*
>
> —Jo Coombs, chief executive, OgilvyOne UK[35]

MAKING IT PERSONAL

If you're a marketing director, running your department as though it were a hypergrowth business requires a new set of personal skills. If you're going to create agile, fast-paced marketing, you personally have to also be flexible and adaptable. You can't allow yourself to fall in love with certain ideas or strategies, and you have to let go of your ego's inclination to be right. Instead, you have to adjust quickly to new situations as they arise. You have to quickly let go of plans that don't work and try something new. There's no room for a big ego in today's marketing director. If you think as the CEO of a hypergrowth business does, then the only thing you care about is what is working. This means you have to become comfortable with letting the marketplace drive your decision making. This takes humility, focus, and objectivity.

It also takes energy. I know this firsthand: having the rapid-response agility of a cuttlefish marketer can get tiring. You must think and rethink, constantly tinker and test, and continuously fine-tune. You can never put things on autopilot. You can never just sit back for a while and allow yourself to just see how it goes. Every day is a battle. The good thing about that is that your job is never boring. The instant feedback as to what works and what doesn't keeps your work exciting.

There's no denying, though, that hypergrowth businesses present huge challenges to the people who run them. Recently, a colleague of mine, Cameron Herold, a business coach and author who has built three $100 million businesses, said to me, "You know, Scott, a lot of times when you come into a curve, most people's immediate reaction is to slow down. But when you talk to racecar drivers, they'll tell you that the curve is the time when they speed up because they've got to power through it. Navigating a small company around the curve into hypergrowth is a lot like that. You can't get scared and slow down. You have to put your foot on the gas and go even faster." That's really good advice, not only for CEOs but also for marketing directors.

Another personal quality that comes in useful for marketing directors is paranoia. When it comes to hypergrowth businesses, the title of my favorite Andrew Grove book says it best: only the paranoid survive. You have to always be aware that your competitors are out there trying to pull ahead of you on the racecourse. As a marketing director, you will be energized by a little paranoia, so you can speed up as you go around those curves.

"Work like there is someone working twenty-four hours a day to take it all away from you."

—Mark Cuban[36]

THE SUBSETS OF CUTTLEFISH AGILITY

The marketplace is a dynamic, shifting arena where critical decisions have to be made in milliseconds. James Dyson understands that and adapts himself and his company accordingly. As marketers, we too must cultivate the same cuttlefish agility. We must build our departments the way Dyson has built his company.

Our ability to do this depends on the traits we'll cover in the next four chapters: an in-depth understanding of what IT can do for marketing; the use of data to create transparency, accountability, and fast learning; active involvement rather than outsourcing decisions; and building a team with varied skill sets. All four of these are what make agility possible. It goes the other way around as well: running your department as a hypergrowth business will radically shape how you do each of these four things.

"What do companies want from today's marketers? They want marketers who take action and don't get caught up in six-month strategy plans. . . . They're looking for rapid prototyping, with fast failure and quick adjustment loops. They want marketers who can build partnerships with key players in other functions and with external partners. . . . They want marketers

*who are manic about solving consumer problems
and a willingness to break some rules to get there.
When you boil it all down, they are looking
for 'marketing entrepreneurs.'"*

—Patrick Spenner, *Forbes*[37]

KEY POINTS TO REMEMBER

→ Modern marketing executives need to run their departments as though they were hypergrowth businesses.

→ Hypergrowth businesses are agile.

→ Marketing agility is the speed at which you can adjust your process to identify and deliver customer value—and make more money.

→ Being agile means being rapidly responsive to consumers, trends, and what is working.

→ Cuttlefish marketers have to be willing to change themselves in order to make their departments function as agile, hypergrowth businesses.

→ Agility encompasses the other four traits of the cuttlefish marketer—and the other four traits all contribute to agility.

CHAPTER 3

TRAIT #2: DIRECT YOUR TECHNOLOGY

UNDERSTAND THE IMPORTANT ROLE TECH PLAYS IN MARKETING

The cuttlefish is a neurological wonder. It has the highest brain-to-body-size ratio of any invertebrate, and its nervous system is capable of conveying subtle and sophisticated messages. I'm not saying that cuttlefish are so intellectually inclined that they're likely to become the star attractions at aquarium shows, but they do need to be savvy if they want to eat. As hunters, they use advanced cognitive skills—including the ability to count[38]—to make constant judgments about which prey is worth targeting. Their rapid response to their environments relies on neurons that pick up messages from their surroundings, instantly carry those messages to the brain, and then transmit impulses and information back to the rest of the body. If we compare cuttlefish neurology to the IT necessary to run today's marketing departments—well, let's just say if you had an IT system that functioned even half as effectively as a cuttlefish's nervous system, you'd be in really good shape.

Unfortunately, IT and marketing departments traditionally have different views and different roles. IT folks and marketing folks speak a different language. They don't always understand each other's priorities. Sometimes they find it difficult to work together. Marketers want advice and recommendations and IT wants input and direction.

Well, too bad. As marketing executives, we really don't have the option of not getting along with IT. Refusing to do so would make as much sense as a cuttlefish that refused to engage with its nervous system. (The cuttlefish that did that would be dead, of course—but that's not far off from what the marketer is who resists IT.) We can no longer understand and respond to our customers without using a significant amount of technology.

To execute in today's marketing environment, we must have technology at our disposal. As marketing executives, we're expected to intimately understand our customers and their behaviors and needs in order to improve the relationship between our brand and consumers. Technology is the nervous system that makes all that possible. It's what allows us to be cuttlefish marketers who are fast, innovative, and agile.

THE NEW IT

Remember the Jujyfruits, Lemonheads, Fireballs, and Atomic Baked Beans of your childhood? They're all made by Ferrara Candy, a company that's been around since 1908. Recently, this old-fashioned company leapt into the twenty-first century when it merged its IT and marketing teams to make its brands more appealing to the millennial generation.

According to Ferrara's CIO, Kristina Paschall, the first step was to bring website management in-house. The company relaunched its website at the same time that it began redesigning a dozen brands and boosting its social media presence. "We need to interact with our consumers through the channels that they interact in," Paschall told CIO.com.[39]

Ferrara's marketing and IT teams have developed a friendly and productive collaboration that's hard for companies to achieve when the deeply entrenched power struggles between marketing and IT get in the way of their working together. According to Paschall, her company has an advantage here because it recreated itself in 2012 when it merged with Farley and Sathers. In effect, the company is now a "$1 billion start-up," freed from old traditions and ready to create fresh strategies for the twenty-first century.

To make this happen, Paschall and her team met regularly with Jamie Mattikow, the chief commercial officer; Jill Manchester, the senior vice president of marketing and brand strategy; and Shanna Kranz, the social media and marketing manager. They all knew that the candy market has come a long way since the days when kids took trips to the candy store and moms made impulse buys standing in the line at supermarkets. But now they had to better understand the modern market. Using data analysis (which we're going to talk about more in the next chapter), Ferrara found that 50 percent of its product portfolio appealed most to people who were thirty years of age and under, the same people who have grown up with social media and prefer to interact with brands online. With input from the marketing teams, Ferrara's IT department replaced outdated landing pages and integrated them with social media. Doing all that in-house, rather than letting an agency do it, reduced overall costs and made their work more agile since IT and marketing could interact in real time to make changes and updates as needed. At the beginning of 2016, Ferrara's new website was ready to roll. It featured a card-style layout that played well on almost any web browser running on PCs, smartphones, and tablets. According to Kranz, it's all designed to appeal to "millennial moms who are always on the phone and tablets."[40]

Ferrara's IT–marketing marriage demonstrates the new role of IT in today's marketing world. In the past, corporate IT teams built and managed companies' tech infrastructure to handle basic business processes such as accounting, billing, ERP, e-mail, phone systems, order-to-cash work flows, and a few business applications such as customer relationship management (CRM) systems. IT "kept the lights on" in the company by ensuring cybersecurity, reducing costs, supporting end users, and managing the business's core transaction systems. Taking care of this complicated network of physical hardware and software kept IT teams busy. As a result, they often saw this as their primary work, and additional projects pushed their way from the marketing department were considered secondary to their priorities.

Meanwhile, marketing departments traditionally acted as the brand's steward. They focused on creative campaigns that generated consumers' excitement and interest for the company's products or services. From the marketers' point of view, the IT department sometimes seemed to be more of a roadblock than a helpful internal resource partner (although I have had some great partnerships with my IT teams in several jobs).

As Ferrara has proved, that scenario can change—and it *needs* to change. Software-as-a-service (SaaS) and cloud-based platforms such as HubSpot and Salesforce have freed up some of IT departments' time, allowing them to shift their focus to other critical technology initiatives. Today, in a world where the Internet has become not only a significant market in itself but also a way to engage and understand your customers, the accuracy, speed, and precision of IT systems can mean the difference between winning and losing customers and market share.

This means that marketing executives in the twenty-first century must follow Ferrara's example and leverage technology to improve customer experience and drive sales growth. To do this, they'll have to rely on tech departments for web- and data-driven marketing activities, such as behavioral targeting and demographic tracking.

Here's a list of just some of the ways in which marketing and technology are now linked, with examples of specific tech tools for each:

- o **Web analytics** tools allow you to collect data on channels, technologies, social media outreach, ads, and offers. Examples: Google Analytics, Adobe Analytics, Ensighten.

- o **Conversion optimization** gets people who come to your website (or wherever you are engaging with them) to do what you want them to do as much as possible. Examples: Wordstream's free Landing Page Grader; Optimizely lets you run A/B tests on landing pages and other website elements; Unbounce lets you test landing pages.

- o **E-mail** that delivers valuable content tailored to your customers' interests can be an effective way to stay in touch with your market. Examples: MailChimp, Constant Contact.

o **Search engine marketing** includes both paid search ads such as Google AdWords, and search engine optimization (SEO) to try to get high organic search listings for your website content. Examples: Google AdWords, Bing and Yahoo, WordStream, Wordtracker, BrightEdge.

o **Remarketing** happens when a company whose website you have visited presents its ads on other websites you visit. It's a cost-effective strategy because a company only advertises to people who have already expressed enough interest in its products or services to come to its site. Examples: Google AdWords remarketing, AdRoll, Perfect Audience.

o **Mobile** phones are now where half of all e-mails are opened and half of all Internet searches will soon be done. This means you should have a website that's easy to read and use on a phone. IT departments have a couple of choices when it comes to making that happen, either designing two versions of your site, one for computer screens and one for phones, or making your site adaptable to either size screen, which is called responsive design.

o **Marketing automation** brings it all together by including analytics, online forms, tracking what people do when they come to your website, personalizing website content, managing e-mail campaigns, facilitating the alignment of sales and marketing through lead scoring and automated alerts to sales people, informing these activities with data from your CRM and third party sources, and more. Examples: HubSpot, Act-On, InfusionSoft, Marketo, and Adobe Campaign.

The CMO Council has found that more than a third of CMOs believe digital marketing will account for 75 percent or more of their spending within the next five years. With so many marketing tools now requiring tech expertise—everything from website optimization to search engine ads, from mobile apps to interactive websites—we require a more seamless way to interact with our IT teammates. In the modern marketing world, IT is truly as essential to our overall success and well-being as a cuttlefish's nervous system is to its survival.

NOT ONLY WHAT BUT HOW

When I compare IT support to a nervous system, I'm not saying that technology changes only *what* we do; it also transforms *how* we do it. It's an organic change, integral to our entire function.

How we develop our marketing data management and reporting platform at MSIGHTS is a good example of the *how*. Our business juxtaposes the methodology of software development with effective marketing strategy. We use Scrum, a form of agile development that many software companies use, and we apply it to our marketing, as well as our software development.

The traditional software development methodology is called Waterfall. It's a linear approach that reminds me of old-style marketing techniques. If you're a software company using Waterfall as you create a product for a customer, you get the job and then you disappear for a year or more while you work your collective butts off until you're ready for the big reveal at the end of the whole process. In the meantime, first you gathered and documented your requirements, then you designed, and after that, you did the coding and user testing, followed by system testing and acceptance testing. After all *that*, you fixed any issues that the testing revealed, and finally, you delivered the finished product. As I said, it's a lot like the way marketing used to work, as we've already described in earlier chapters.

Scrum development, a term that comes from the game of rugby, is totally different from Waterfall. Instead, it might look something like this: a customer creates a prioritized wish list, and during planning, the development team pulls a small chunk from the top of that wish list and decides how to implement those pieces. The team then has a relatively short period of time, usually two to four weeks, to complete its work. This fast-paced, small-scale development is called a sprint. During the sprint, the team meets each day in what's known as a daily scrum to assess its progress. At the end of the sprint, the work should be ready to put out into the market while the team chooses the next chunk from the wish list and begins a new sprint.

Developed in the late 1990s by Ken Schwaber and Jeff Sutherland, Scrum creates a system that lets people manage complex problems using whatever processes and techniques work best for them while still maintaining productivity and consistency. Scrum breaks down work into pieces so you're continuously delivering product to the market in an extremely agile way. The process itself allows developers to gain new information, which they can then apply to their next sprint, creating product that is constantly adapting to real-world demands.

In the old days, for example, if you were a software developer, you had to ship out CDs and wait for the response. Now, at MSIGHTS, I can quickly launch a feature and get instant feedback, both directly from users and by looking at usage statistics. This gives me the incentive to release often so we can get a lot of new features into market and see what users like and use and then capitalize on it.

Today's agile marketing is so integrated with IT that it comes naturally to use the same vocabulary and methodologies. In fact, when most people hear the phrase *agile marketing*, they usually think of the Scrum methodology. Scrum provides a framework that creates a culture of transparency and accountability (which we'll be talking about more in the next chapter).

The Scrum framework when it's applied to marketing looks like this:

o **Sprints:** Marketing sprints are projects, such as marketing / media plans, or creative refreshes, with specific goals and deadlines. They shouldn't last any longer than a month, and two weeks is really ideal. Smaller teams may be able to handle one-week sprints. The ideal sprint team size for software development is three to nine people, according to *The Scrum Guide*.[41] Andrea Fryrear's *Guide to Using Scrum Methodology for Agile Marketing* allows this number to be increased to twelve people for a marketing scrum but recommends not going any higher.[42] The good thing about this is that when you have sprints going on all the time, you're going to get wins every few weeks, which is great for morale and momentum. When failures happen, which they always do and marketers should embrace and learn from, you've only lost a few weeks of work, and now you can move on to trying and testing something else.

o **Sprint Planning:** At the planning meeting, you identify what you want to achieve and figure out how you can get it done. This has to be a precisely defined objective. It can't be something vague, such as "improve our social media presence." It's easier to use if you're a software developer; you can use Scrum to define improvements and product features. As marketers, we may have a harder time identifying a measureable goal. We should keep in mind that a sprint's goal must be something that can be definitively achieved within the short span of time we've allotted for the sprint. Part of the planning meeting will be defining what constitutes *done* for that particular sprint. Don't let it become a moving target. You can always come back to it in a future sprint.

o **Daily Scrum:** This is a daily, fifteen-minute mini-meeting to discuss progress and hurdles. Each team member gets a turn to say what she contributed to the sprint goal yesterday and what she plans to do today. Equally important, the team member can share what roadblocks or dependencies she has so they can be removed.

o **Sprint Review:** Once the sprint is over, the team gets together to discuss what was achieved during the sprint and its impact on future projects awaiting implementation in the backlog, a long list of things that still have to be done. The sprint review should include a discussion of what was completed and what was not; what went well and what didn't; and what problems were solved. The team leader then presents remaining backlog items, and the groups discusses what should come next, which will eventually lead to the next sprint planning meeting. This is also the time to review any changes in the marketplace that could impact future sprint goals, as well as any budget or timeline constraints that the team will face.

○ **Sprint Retrospective:** The final piece of Scrum is a meeting in which the team inspects itself and its processes for opportunities to improve. This should happen after the sprint review but before the next sprint planning meeting, which has the purpose of evaluating speed, estimating planning activities, and defining user stories.

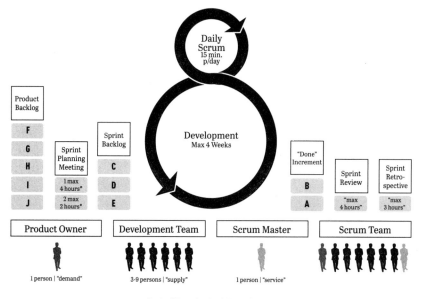

Scrum is an extremely useful methodology for marketing. Like most agile practices that have their roots in software development, however, it can't be simply imported whole into your marketing department. Use whatever works. Don't try to fit marketing's round peg into IT's square hole.

COORDINATING IT AND MARKETING SPRINTS

At MSIGHTS, we're aware of the differences between tech teammates and marketing teammates. At the same time, though, we've found that despite the differences, marketing sprints and IT sprints are functionally similar. Development and innovation is cyclic and iterative, driving ever-evolving experimentation in response to customer feedback. Innovation happens fast and it shifts directions quickly as necessary.

If you take a look at a different type of business, you can see how this looks from another perspective. Carsurfing is a start-up company that offers an app for finding rides to and from events such as concerts. It matches up people who need transportation with people who can offer rides. None of it works without IT working alongside marketing. According to Ben Watson, the CMO of marketing software vendor WhatsNexx and advisor to Carsurfing, "We're combining marketing, technology, and the creative process into one set of iterations. We're building the look and feel of the website, the customer journey, [and] our knowledge of persona into the product design and content at the same time."[43]

A specific example of how this approach works happened as Carsurfing was first developing its IT system. As the IT people imported events listed on Facebook into the Carsurfing platform, they noticed a spike connected to the Burning Man festival. IT immediately reported the spike and everyone dropped everything to focus on getting people to Burning Man. The process looked a whole lot like cuttlefish neurology that picks up a message from the environment, gets it to the brain, and triggers instantaneous responses throughout the entire organism.

The Carsurfing team built a dedicated landing page for Facebook users who were going to Burning Man, and they validated their internal IT systems, their marketing approach, and their user interface, all in one cycle.[44] Notice that there was no long development period, followed by a big unveiling. Instead, it was a single seamless process. By incorporating customer feedback into IT development, both marketing and the product itself hit their mark.

Integrating IT and marketing through Scrum methodology does have its challenges, however, as the Netherlands consulting company Xebia found out when it worked with ING to implement Scrum across both the IT and marketing departments. Xebia discovered that the two departments spoke a different language, and their personalities and temperaments tended to be quite different from each other. The IT people at ING were accustomed to using technical terms; they asked a lot of questions and they wanted things to be very clear before they started. Meanwhile, the ING marketers wanted only a short explanation, and then they were eager to get going. Xebia coaches concluded that marketers were more likely to be extroverts who were comfortable with learning by doing and taking the initiative. Each side, the coaches concluded, could learn from the other's strengths. So long as the differences were acknowledged and identified, the process of working together made both sides more effective at their roles.[45]

Whatever your business is, I'm confident you too can benefit from integrating your marketing approach with your technology. Let's say you're the marketer for a chain of restaurants. Your places may be the hot thing right now, but that could change completely next month. If you have a good IT partner, you'll be able to spot shifts in your customers' preferences as they happen and quickly adjust both your menu and your marketing accordingly. Remember that if you're the person in charge of marketing, you're not only directing your IT but also integrating marketing with your entire business, using the mind-set of a hypergrowth business person to drive everything you do.

That sounds good, right? Except that the fast-paced flexibility we're talking about can feel uncomfortable, even to marketing extroverts. It's contrary to human nature. After all, we're not really cuttlefish, and none of this is instinctual. Marketing executives' training is probably in marketing, not technology, and also, it's human nature to feel uncomfortable with the unknown. As marketers, we're not accustomed to relying on IT in the organic way a cuttlefish relies on its nervous system. Instead, we've seen technology and marketing as two separate functions, and now we're not only being asked to play nice with each other; we're expected to somehow merge some of our functions into a new organism.

ACT AS LICHEN DO

When it comes to living creatures, the cuttlefish is a pretty odd one. It looks a little like some space alien, with weird eyes and many tentacles. In the botanical world, a lichen is another odd organism. In almost all cases, however, that greenish-gray leathery stuff you find on rocks and old stumps isn't a very good analogy for what we're talking about in this book. So don't worry. I'm not going to recommend that we all become lichen marketers, because lichen really never does much of anything. But lichen does have an interesting feature we might consider imitating when we think about our relationship with IT: lichens are actually two organisms that have joined together to become a single living unit.

Until fairly recently, scientists had no idea how lichen could survive in all the places where it did, including bare rocks in the far north. In the nineteenth century, some scientists even thought that lichen proved that given enough time, stone was able to change into a living thing.[46] Turns out, though, that a lichen can grow even in inhospitable places because it contains both fungi and algae. Fungi, which cannot harvest light energy from the sun because they lack chlorophyll, join with algae, which do contain chlorophyll, and together, they become one of the hardiest visible organisms on Earth.[47] The fungus is the dominant member of the relationship, but it couldn't continue to exist without the energy the algae provide. Together, they thrive in environments where neither one alone would be able to survive.

Lichen's fungi-algae relationship is the analogy I strive for to achieve the necessary relationship between today's marketing departments and IT. Where once we thought of IT as an add-on to marketing, now it's formed a symbiotic relationship that's so intertwined with marketing as to be inseparable. The marketing department may be the dominant one (in my opinion), but its very existence and future success depends on IT. You can't pull the two apart. They're a single, meshed entity. Today's marketing couldn't exist without all the things that IT does: website creation; digital analytics for feedback; social media, interactive content, and mobile apps for media channels; marketing automation; and CRM. Pull out these IT strands from a marketing department, and you'd be left with—well, not much. As I said earlier, a cuttlefish without its nervous system would just not survive.

This has practical implications for marketing directors. I discovered this firsthand back in 2004, when I founded MSIGHTS, Inc. My idea had been to create a technology company that would offer marketers the performance data and transparency they required to thrive in today's data-driven marketing world. The services MSIGHTS offers to marketing departments aren't supplementary and dispensable; they're essential to the very life and function of modern marketing success. I understood that before I started the company, but what I also learned very quickly was that the challenges of creating great technology and the challenges of creating great marketing share a whole lot of similarities. Running a SaaS technology company, I discovered, is a lot like running a marketing department.

For those of us who started our careers prior to the world's digital tsunami, that statement may seem counterintuitive. After all, traditionally, the model marketing person and the stereotypical IT person have different functions on the professional spectrum. But that's not true any longer. If you're a marketing director today, the art of managing your department increasingly resembles the art of managing IT (and arguably vice versa).

That may not always seem like a comfortable fit. If you're trained and experienced in old-style marketing, you may feel you're venturing into unfamiliar territory whenever you try to integrate technology with what you've always done. If that's the case, keep in mind that the mental map you're using is no longer accurate. You're thinking that marketing and technology live in two separate territories, with boundaries between them, then what you should be doing is seeing them as a single symbiotic organism. The marketing mind and the IT mind are no longer separated and distinct. Both now must creatively interact within a constantly shifting kaleidoscope of digitally powered interactions in order to produce innovative experiences in complex environments that are intensely competitive.

I'm not saying that every marketer has to understand complicated coding and other high-end, complex IT functions. Within lichen, the fungus still doesn't carry out photosynthesis, and the algae haven't become identical with the fungus any more than marketers and IT folks have exactly the same skills and abilities. I've run a technology company for more than a decade, but that doesn't mean I now comprehend all the ins and outs of what we do on the database architecture or in our software coding.

I don't have to understand that (luckily we have an amazing team of engineers who do). What I should grasp, though, is the bigger picture so that I can make sure that our team is building the right platforms for scalability, flexibility, and all the other things our marketing users need—and want. As the director of a marketing department, you too should be able to oversee the entire integrated organism that you're running. You can't see IT as something separate from everything else you do. Instead, you need to not only embrace IT but also be able to direct its essential and organic functions within your department.

> *"Today IT and marketing represent the 'yin and yang,' two seemingly contradictory forces that actually complement each other."*
>
> —Adobe[48]

BE THE PITCHER, NOT THE CATCHER

Turning from the world of biology to sports, another analogy I find helpful is that of a baseball catcher and a pitcher. Catchers and pitchers have to work together; you can't have one without the other. They work as a team, with the catcher feeding signals to the pitcher that help the pitcher to carry out his or

IT director   *Marketing executive*

her role. Ultimately, however, it's the pitcher who throws the ball. As the marketing director, you'll work with IT personnel. You'll rely on their feedback and input. But you want to make sure you're the one who throws the ball.

In the real-life world of marketing, this has financial implications. Today's marketing departments have tech budgets that are as big as, if not bigger than, IT's budgets. This is because the close relationship between marketing operations and IT can be pretty visible to data-savvy marketers, whereas the IT department may not have as clear a vision of its practical application in powering marketing. As a marketing executive, you will likely spend more on technology than the CIO does because you're using software-mediated channels to engage your audience. Because the marketing executive is responsible for that outcome, it makes sense that you should take a leadership role in the technology strategy to achieve it.

This means that if you outsource your marketing IT to an outside partner, such as Accenture (which is an amazing company) or your ad agency, you shouldn't expect that partner to make all your decisions for you. You don't want your company's internal IT department making all your marketing technology (martech) decisions either. After all, they're not the ones who are the experts in really understanding how different technologies should be deployed to run and optimize marketing programs. Remember you're the pitcher, not the catcher. Just because technology is so embedded in everything you do that you can't unwind it, doesn't mean outside marketing groups or partners should make all the decisions.

IT CHOICES

As the director of marketing, you know the goals you have to achieve, so you are the best person to plug your technology—whether it's web and mobile marketing apps, marketing automation, webinar and virtual event software, personalization, or interactive ads, just to name a few—into your company's marketing.

Don't make the mistake of thinking that marketing technology's job is only to make your existing processes more efficient. Marketing automation that schedules batch-and-blast e-mail, for example, can make an existing process more efficient, but the bigger opportunity here is to create a better e-mail experience for your potential customers and prospects. And in many cases, IT can help you create entirely new kinds of processes that weren't even possible before you joined forces with your tech department. Just as the cuttlefish's nervous system is its interface between the world "out there" and its internal reactions, marketing technol-ogy can also be the interface by which you see and touch the digital world. Your choice of martech and how you use it will shape the experiences you deliver to your market.

marketing strategy   technology

With that said, don't fall into the mistake of thinking that every shiny piece of adtech or martech that comes along will be the answer to your marketing problems. Before you invest in technology, make sure it matches up with a marketing strategy and that you have a clear ROI target in mind from the technology. This doesn't mean that your strategy should define tech investments. In other words, don't figure out a strategy and then go looking for software to implement it. Nor should your tech drive your strategy.

In other words, don't create a strategy to use a particular feature of your software just because you happen to have that technology.

Steve Jobs once said, "People don't know what they want until you show it to them," and along the same lines, Henry Ford said, "If I had asked people what they wanted, they would have said faster horses." What these two famous quotes say to the technology–marketing relationship is this: tech and marketing development must coexist in a circular process that allows new tech to emerge alongside equally new marketing applications. As Scott Brinker, author of the *Chief Marketing Technologist* blog (chiefmartec.com) and the great book *Hacking Marketing* says, "If marketing doesn't really understand technology—and IT doesn't really understand marketing—then their 'collaboration' can all too easily look like this: Marketing asks for faster horses. IT gives them faster horses. The automobile passes both of them by."[49]

Scott Brinker describes a circular relationship between tech and marketing. New advances in technology, he says, will shape your strategy development; your strategy guides where and how you invest in tech; as you use that tech, you then refine and reshape your strategy, which sends you back around the cycle. This ongoing cycle can keep your company innovative, agile, competitive, and constantly growing in response to your market.

To go back to the baseball analogy, teams require both pitcher and catcher. In the tech–marketing relationship, you, as a marketing executive, must make sure your department adheres to IT governance in terms of security, regulatory requirements, and integration with the rest of the company's IT systems. At the same time, you have to "own" IT in the sense that you take charge of it; you bring it within the scope of what you oversee.

KNOW ENOUGH TO KNOW WHAT YOU'RE DOING

In the last chapter, we said you should run your marketing department as though it were a hypergrowth business. Being able to do that connects directly to being the "pitcher" of your technology. If you can't direct your IT, you won't be able to run your department as though it were a hypergrowth business. You won't be able to achieve that cuttlefish agility. Your IT must act as a nervous system that drives the entire business so that it can achieve return on marketing investment (ROMI).

If you're not able to oversee IT at that level, you're going to end up chasing shiny things that sound great but may not be what you really need. Somebody says to you, "Have you done an attribution study?" and you say, "Shoot! I guess I'd better do an attribution study," even though you don't know what the heck it is or how it can benefit you. Someone else gives you a checklist, and you think you'd better get started checking off those boxes. You don't have a clue *why* you need to check them all off; you just feel you should do them so you look good. That is not how to run a hypergrowth business. You should be able to understand your IT enough to make intelligent decisions about your business needs. And to do all that, you must be willing to let go of old ways of doing things.

KNOWING WHEN TO JUMP SHIP

When you've had a good ride in the ship you've been sailing, it's pretty scary to jump ship, even if you can see there's a storm coming. To jump ship is sometimes considered a bad thing to do. It implies that you don't have the necessary commitment and courage to stick it out for the long haul. Or it means that the ship you're on is going down fast and you have to get off before you drown. I think of this figure of speech a little differently, though. In my mind, there's a long flotilla of "ships" out there, and you have to decide which one you want to be on.

Let's say you're in a canoe that's done a good job, so far, of carrying you down the stream, but now the stream has merged with a larger river, the water's gotten rough, and there's a big boat up ahead that's far more capable of navigating the rolling water. In fact, it will even take advantage of the fast-moving current to reach its destination sooner. Doesn't it make sense to climb out of the small craft you've been in and get on board that larger boat? The canoe did a great job on the little stream, but it's not built for what lies ahead.

You could feel attached to that little canoe, though. After all, it's the only boat you've ever rowed in, and it feels comfortable. The larger boat up ahead is a big unknown. And you feel a sense of loyalty to that little canoe.

But does it really make sense to try to paddle out into a raging river when you could get out of the canoe and climb on board the larger boat? Let's say you ride that big boat all the way to the ocean, and now you're trying to navigate the surf when you see an ocean liner. The smart move would be to jump ship again. Go with what works best for the situation in which you find yourself. The other boats got you where you had to go. Now it's time to move on.

> *"He who rejects change is the architect of decay. The only human institution which rejects progress is the cemetery."*
>
> —Harold Wilson

Working with IT is a lot like that. By its very nature, today's technology is constantly changing. Just when you think you've mastered a software application, the maker releases another version. With cloud-based programs, the upgrades just keep coming, faster and faster. So you'd better not get too attached to any particular "boat" you've been sailing.

At MSIGHTS, every time we finish a two-week sprint and start another one, it's like jumping ship. We have to be able to let go of what worked last time and find what works *this* time. Sure, we have our long-range course charted out, but every time we change boats, we know we'll have to adjust the map.

Okay, so where are you, the marketing director, in this analogy I've been building? You're the one who is making the decision to jump ships, and once on board, you're the captain. Keep in mind, though, that no one expects that every time you climb aboard a larger boat, you'll head down to the engine room and start tinkering with whatever propels the ship. You don't have to get your degree in marine engineering. But people do expect you to be the one who chooses the voyage's direction, the North Star so to speak. You don't have to understand every single bit of how the engine operates; you just have to know enough about what's happening to piece it all together into an overall course.

Even that can be intimidating. As you move from boat to boat, everything becomes that much more complex. If you are really good at paddling a canoe, it can be tempting to just keep on paddling instead of taking on the risk and responsibility of captaining a far larger craft. It seems safer. You may even feel you'll look less foolish as an expert at canoeing—even in a canoe in the middle of a storm at sea—than you would trying to captain an ocean liner. But really, that little canoe just can't survive out there in the ocean.

So get used to jumping ship fast. A larger, more complex boat will be along any minute, one that can take you and your team exactly where you want to go. You'll expect the folks down in the engine room to keep things functioning smoothly, but you're still the captain. You don't need the so-called experts to set your course.

> *"The power of fear is quite tremendous in evolving oneself to think and act differently today, and to ask questions today that we weren't asking about our roles before. And it's that mind-set change—from an expert-based mind-set to one that is much more dynamic and much more learning oriented, as opposed to a fixed mind-set—that I think is fundamental to the sustainable health of any company, large, small, or medium."*

—Murli Buluswar, Chief Science Officer, AIG

DON'T ALWAYS TRUST THE EXPERTS

I'm not really saying I have anything against IT and technology experts. They're the lifeblood of our company, after all, and they're intelligent and creative in ways I'll never be. The technology they build can do impressive things for a marketing department, things that are absolutely essential in today's world. But what IT experts don't always understand is marketing itself.

My former client and business colleague Damien Cummings, a marketing leader who's currently global head of digital marketing at Standard Chartered Bank in Singapore, defines the business of marketing as "mapping out where the company/product is today, then looking at the short-term goals (quarterly, annual) and the long term goals (2 years+) to see what the brand value, sales, market share, profit and customer satisfaction is going to look like."[50] In other words, if you're the marketing director, you're the captain of the ship who charts the course ahead.

Cummings breaks down his definition further, saying that marketing has four roles: (1) helping set these objectives (internally with senior management, sales, product and support teams), (2) building a plan to get there, (3) reporting on the progress toward the goals, and (4) putting in place the right marketing capability (people, process, platforms and partners) to support the brand's growth. Tech people, Cummings says, "only focus on the capability piece and neglect almost all of the other areas."[51] The reason for this disconnect is that they're pushing their products—software—as the answer to marketing challenges, while not understanding the marketer's context and objectives. Cummings points to social intelligence/social listening as a good example of technology that IT people often push. It's a great technology, one that can offer real benefit to a marketing department. But as a marketing director, before you sign on to use social intelligence, you'd better be able to say exactly what problem it solves for you. Will it help you make more sales? And if so, how?

Cummings goes on to say that IT people tend to focus far too much on product features over the specific benefits the product can offer to meet an individual company's requirements. They also neglect "the change management element of all new tech programs. This is critical because it's not just implementing the tech, but it's more important to train staff, get rid of the old tech and previous processes that this solution is replacing, get a new process in place, and update everyone's [key performance indicators]."[52]

Coordinating all these processes is an enormously complex task. You can't rely on the so-called experts to do if for you. You're the only one who has the big picture, the larger perspective that will allow you to fit together all the pieces.

YOU OWN THE PUZZLE PIECES

When you're putting a jigsaw puzzle together, you start out with a hundred, or maybe even a thousand, little pieces that, at first glance, look as though they're completely random shapes and colors. You have the picture on the cover of the box that works as a guide, a map to let you know that all the orange pieces should be over there on the right side of the puzzle, and the blues ones are on top, and the green ones are along the bottom. Even with that information, though, the jumble of pieces can be overwhelming. You need to build the framework using the edge pieces to give yourself the context for the big picture. Once you have the edges connecting all four corners, you'll be able to tackle the rest of the puzzle more easily.

Adtech and martech can seem, to marketers, an immensely intricate puzzle that just keeps getting larger and more complicated every year. That feeling isn't an illusion. Not only are new capabilities and programs being constantly developed but there's also been an explosion of tech companies that offer marketing tech solutions.

Scott Brinker reported that in March 2016 there were 3,874 marketing technology solutions, while just five years earlier, there were only around 150.[53] As vendors proliferate, companies are becoming more and more specialized in an effort to carve out a niche for themselves.

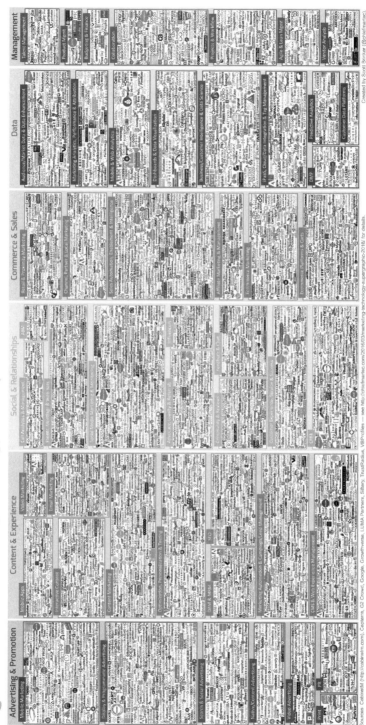

Graphic courtesy of Scott Brinker

The many companies out there make it tempting for a marketing director to rely on one of them—or an assortment of them—for technical direction. Don't. Each of these companies will only be able to offer you a piece of the adtech/martech puzzle. They can't help you assemble the pieces. The pieces they each contribute may be essential to the picture you're trying to put together, but they won't build out the edges of the puzzle. They won't show you where the corners are. You'll have to do that for yourself.

The edges of the puzzle are equivalent to the core four to five pillars of your IT platform, or the "stack." You have to collaborate with your in-house IT staff to get these huge pillars in place to support everything you do. After that, your marketing technologist lead will be able to fill in any gaps with specialized providers.

As the director of your department, you naturally gravitate toward the things you enjoy, which are probably building marketing campaigns and tackling marketing communications challenges. To push the puzzle analogy further, after you finish the edges, you'll put together all the pieces for the central image—the kitten on the lawn or the cottage on the hill—because that's the fun part that comes easily. Meanwhile, you'll leave empty the vast expanse that should be filled in with sky-blue or grass-green pieces because they're just too hard or require too much time. Maybe you'll hope someone else will do that part for you.

Building the edges of a puzzle is relatively easy and straightforward. It takes real commitment and perseverance to fill in the interior image. The same holds true for piecing together the IT that will support your marketing efforts. You can't possibly know all the technological details that go into filling in the spaces between your stack pillars. But you should at least own the pieces. Don't give them away to someone else and expect that person to put them together for you.

Sometimes this comes down to simply being willing to ask questions to help yourself understand the larger picture. If you and IT don't understand the same languages, though, you may not be able to understand the answers you get.

OVERCOMING LANGUAGE BARRIERS

As you go deeper into the big picture for IT, getting into more complex requirements and implementations, having a productive dialogue between marketing and technology providers becomes increasingly difficult. Creative people—the folks who develop marketing content and ad campaign creative ads—don't speak the same language as IT people, who create the technology that carries the content and creative.

If the two perspectives can't connect and interact, the job can't be done well. As a marketing technology solution provider, I know from experience that my customers expect me to plug into their vision. The problem is, though, that they often expect me to simply take over from there, while I want them to be engaged in the entire process, using their vision to guide my company's results. To make this happen, both sides have to be able to communicate with each other so they can build the end product together.

This communication breakdown may look a little different these days when it occurs between creatives and technologists, but the principles are the same. This time, though, it goes the other way: it's the creatives who are not understanding that little changes can throw everything off.

A lot of times our clients want to say, "Here's the end solution I need. Just do it. And then when you're done, I may drop in a few changes here and there, but don't worry, they won't be a big deal." And then what happens? Well, after we've completed the entire implementation, the client comes back and says, "Oh, did I say that element needed to be static? Well, I should have said that we need it to be dynamic. Can you just make that little piece dynamic?" The client doesn't seem to realize what's involved. He doesn't comprehend the huge amount of work we're going to have to redo from that custom implementation.

IT and marketing should work together. That doesn't mean you should go fifty feet deep with your understanding of IT processes. But at least go down a foot, far enough to have some understanding of what's going on down there beneath the surface. Be engaged; be actively involved. Give direction along the way, keeping development on track so it doesn't have to be redone in the end. Your marketing team will be using IT—they're the ones who are closest to the practical requirements—so you must be the one who drives an efficient, on-track development course.

At MSIGHTS, we have the same communication challenge. I'm a marketer. My business partner and coauthor, Ivan Aguilar, is a technologist. We make a strong combination only because we've learned to communicate and work together. We each have to be engaged and interested in the other's perspective. This doesn't require that we meet in the middle. No, we have to go even further than that: we have to both cross over into each other's worlds.

ADOBE'S BEST PRACTICES FOR IMPROVING COMMUNICATIONS BETWEEN MARKETING AND IT

1. **Drive change from the top down.** C-level executives have to prioritize collaboration and invest the time, resources, and money required for it to work.

2. **Share key performance indicators.** The CMO and CIO are responsible for meeting shared objectives, so everyone is invested in the organization's success.

3. **Nurture relationships among teams.** A relationship built on a common objective has a greater likelihood of working out than one with conflicting goals.

4. **Measure your progress.** Measurement is essential for every campaign. Today, an organization can define and measure goals with more precision than it could before.[54]

THE MARKETING DIRECTOR'S SWEET SPOT

Your role as a marketing executive is located where the three circles of a Venn diagram intersect. Each of the three circles has different content, as indicated on the following diagram. That small area you see at the center of the diagram, where the three circles overlap, is where you must function. That's your martech sweet spot.

Odds are good you probably know quite a lot about the strategy and creative part of this diagram. That's fine. Actually, it's great because the more clearly you can articulate what you need—whether that's customized marketing messages or lower costs—the better IT will be able to deliver, and the more you'll be able to stay focused rather than surrendering to the lure of the technology du jour. But you have to have that overlap with technology to make it work.

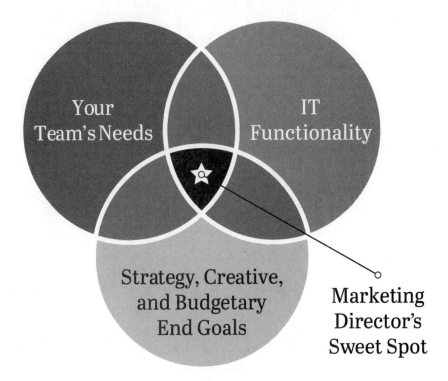

A good way to define your own martech sweet spot is by asking questions. The answers should help you clarify how the pieces of your IT complement each other, whether any are redundant, and what's missing. Questions like that help you and the tech team understand where you'll require the most input.

Let's say we have a new client at MSIGHTS who starts out by saying, "Okay, let me just make sure I understand. What MSIGHTS does is take data from all these different silos, all these different operating platforms, and bring the results data sources into one place, clean them, and merge them so the reporting data are combined, cleansed, and ready for analysis so my team doesn't have to spend a ton of time merging this stuff in Excel. You do it automatically, so we just focus more on reporting analysis. Am I right? Is that what you guys do?"

She's asking a genuine question, but the question itself tells me she already understands how MSIGHTS will fit into the puzzle she's piecing together. She sees what pieces we have to offer that she doesn't already have. And that's great. She's found her martech sweet spot.

On the other hand, a client called me yesterday to say, "I don't really get what you do. I just don't understand what it is you're supposed to be doing for us."

"Okay," I said, "let's talk about your company for a minute. Tell me what your platform does, and then I can explain to you how we can complement that."

"Um," he said, "well . . . I'd have to get our IT tech lead on the phone with you for that. I really don't know what our platform does."

This guy has a problem. How can he run his department if he doesn't even know what the IT department is currently doing for the company?

Being out of touch with any of the three circles will hurt your effectiveness as a marketing executive, but the third circle in our Venn diagram—your team's requirements—is one that often gets overlooked. In other words, what toolkit must your team—whether internal employees or outside agency partners—have to achieve its objectives? This may have to do as much with personalities and emotions as it does with skill sets. For example, a marketing executive recently told me, "Have you met our guy Joe? He's really good at building those Excel reports we use, so we don't need that from you. He does it every Monday, which is why I don't see a need for your company to be doing them. Joe just loves doing them, and he does them well."

But then I talk to Joe, and I hear an entirely different story. "I *hate* managing spreadsheets," he tells me. "I am so bored with Excel. I hate these reports, I hate Mondays, and I'm thinking about quitting. I hate it so much."

Well, clearly, there's a disconnect here between the executive and her team. She's not in the martech sweet spot where she should be, and as a result, she won't be able to drive all the other elements of the entire department as efficiently as she might otherwise. Operating from that martech sweet spot means you'll have to do all the things we've already talked about: be willing to change and let go of the familiar, be agile, ask questions, and try new things.

Remember, though, I'm not saying that you'll have to start going to technology conferences instead of marketing ones, and you won't have to learn to draw those funny-looking database diagrams. Think about it: if you were to draw a diagram of a cuttlefish's neurology and show it to him, do you think he'd have a clue what he was looking at? He just has to *use* his nervous system, not comprehend every technical detail of what makes it function.

And you just have to get enough of an overlap in your proficiency areas to drive the overall vision. The five traits of a cuttlefish marketer, including what we'll talk about next, which is data feedback, will all help to keep you working from that martech sweet spot.

"There's not a marketer out there who doesn't wish they knew more about their customers, but for most brands this is a huge headache due to data silos, proprietary labels, cross-platform identifiers, etc. . . . In today's digital reality, the marketers who 'get it' are at an advantage."

—Brian Ferrario, VP Marketing, Drawbridge[55]

TECHNOLOGIST'S PERSPECTIVE

IVAN AGUILAR, CO-FOUNDER OF MSIGHTS

Technologists like to design new applications and build new and improved systems. We love technology, and the majority of the time we are early adopters. So it comes naturally for us to recommend tools and systems that use the latest technology. It is very easy to detect a product that is designed by technologists because we like to add all the features and all the variations, even if only 1 percent of the users will really need them. In order to direct a technology team, it is best to discuss the strategy and the bigger picture so technology teams don't get distracted with the details (things that are important but not relevant at the strategy conversations). Once the strategy and focus are set, then the teams will do what they do best, which is solving problems. In this case, however, the problems have a meaning in the strategy and not just for the fun of solving the problem.

When we started developing MSIGHTS's platform, we set up the strategy to be a system that provides marketing analytics to users, one in which the users don't spend all day creating them or being distracted by the operational items involved in building the analysis. Scott always kept us lined up with the features we needed to expose to the users so that we always saw the product as an extension of the marketing team to analyze their data and give the team the freedom to go on with their other activities in the day.

We designed the platform to be very flexible in its core because we understood that the analysis isn't static; it evolves and changes all the time. Our platform changes by adding more data points and more sources to look at the numbers from a different perspective, while users drill into the data from different elements depending on how they are reading the data. With this flexibility in mind, we've learned that if a dashboard (reports created to perform an analysis) remains static for a long period of time, it might have lost its relevance, so we've included a lot of statistics to measure "freshness" of the dashboard (execution times, who sees the report, who changes it, etc.). All these metrics give users information to determine if they need to look at some numbers differently. It helps them avoid the "blindness" that can come because they have gotten accustomed to seeing the same things presented the same way.

KEY POINTS TO REMEMBER

→ IT is essential to the cuttlefish marketer's success.

→ IT and marketing need to form a symbiotic relationship that works seamlessly.

→ Scrum methodology is a helpful framework that allows IT and marketing efforts to work together.

→ Technology and marketing strategy interact in a circular relationship where each shapes the other.

→ As a marketing executive, you don't have to become a tech expert to captain your ship, but you should understand enough to be able to set the direction and lead.

→ Language barriers between IT and marketing must be overcome for them to work together effectively.

→ Find your martech sweet spot—the place where IT functionality, your team's requirements, and creative and budgetary end goals intersect—and claim it.

CHAPTER 4

TRAIT #3: ACTIVATE DATA

EMBRACE TRANSPARENCY AND ACCOUNTABILITY IN ORDER TO LEARN AND MOVE FAST

The cuttlefish is constantly collecting visual data. Its eyes are incredibly receptive to light, starting when the creature is still in the egg, and unlike human beings, it has no blind spots. We humans all have metaphorical blind spots—areas in our lives where we simply can't perceive reality—but we also have literal blind spots on our retinas where the optic nerve enters the eyeball. Cuttlefish's retinas, however, are fully responsive to light across their entire surface. In fact, scientists have discovered that cuttlefish can actually see the angle at which light is reflected. In a recent study, the researcher Shelby Temple reported that cuttlefish sensitivity to light data is far more sophisticated than scientists had originally suspected. Previously, they believed that cuttlefish's perception of polarization (the angle of light) was limited to differences of about ten to twenty degrees, but they found that cuttlefish could actually detect differences as small as one degree.[56] This data is extremely useful to the cuttlefish because it allows the creature to respond to the slightest changes in its environment, activating its considerable array of hunting mechanisms.

In other words, cuttlefish don't just collect data; for them data collection and instant response are inseparably linked. This isn't something they turn on and off for various circumstances; it's an ongoing, continuous process that allows them to be successful predators. As a marketing executive, you must cultivate a similar sensitivity to data. Just as a cuttlefish's nervous system would do it little good without a system for collecting information from its environment, your IT is only as effective as the data you feed into it.

Data has nothing to do with emotions. It simply is what it is. Humans, however, can't help but have emotional reactions. When we're in love with an idea, it's easy to feel defensive when we encounter feedback telling us that idea might not be as brilliant as we'd supposed. We may resist holding ourselves accountable to cold, dry statistics, and we may find ourselves obfuscating the real results of a campaign to make our ideas look more successful than they really are. It's human nature to think like that. Unlike human beings, however, cuttlefish aren't prone to getting emotionally attached to a course of action, nor do they keep doing things simply because they've always done them that way. Their movements and other behaviors are always triggered by the data their eyes (and other sensors) pick up from their environment.

Your department should be as organically linked to data as a cuttlefish is. In today's world, relying on data can't be regarded as an add-on to the marketing process any more than technology can be.

Both are as integral to marketing as a nervous system and light data are to a cuttlefish. Data is what empowers you and your department, giving you the information you should have to be flexible and fast. When you activate data, embracing transparency and accountability, you can learn fast and move fast—as a cuttlefish does.

> *"Data science is not voodoo. We are not building fancy math models for their own sake. We are trying to listen to what the customer is telling us through their behavior."*
>
> —Kevin Geraghty, VP of Reporting and Analytics, 360i[57]

DATA, MARKETING, AND PRODUCT DEVELOPMENT

A few years ago, the marketer Julia Porter transformed the UK's *Guardian* News and Media into a cuttlefish marketing machine. At the time, the brand was beset with difficulties. Internet news sources and social media were dominating the market, and revenue streams from the *Guardian's* print circulation were rapidly declining.[58] Porter knew that if the newspaper were to survive, it would have to make enormous changes, becoming far more agile in its response to readers—and data was the key that allowed her to achieve this.

In an era when the public tends to fear Big Brother watching them through their digital data, Porter had to first educate customers about why the paper needed their input. She launched a company charter titled *Why Your Data Matters* with a video explaining how customers' data would be used to make the newspaper more useful to them. By involving its newspaper readers in data collection right from the start, Guardian News and Media magnified and empowered its data collection. In a recent periodical article, Porter said, "It felt to me that we did something quite innovative with that video and it took a lot of effort to get to that point because it got us talking about the importance about being transparent with our customers."[59]

The video was just the first step in the company's transformation into a cuttlefish marketing engine. The depth of information the company ended up acquiring enabled it to build a powerful data-based model that determined what was said to whom, when, where, and how.

Understanding its different audiences' profiles and preferences allowed the *Guardian* to create better products, while making its advertising more effective. Like a cuttlefish's sensitive visual sensors, the paper's data collection was so finely tuned that it could now effectively target various segments of its readership. "If you are able to marry up transactions and behavioural data with attitudes and demographic data," Porter explained, "then you will be able to understand what life stage people are at, what they are interested in buying and how they will respond to messages."[60] For example, some people were likely candidates for digital subscription packs, while others responded well to advertisements for books and holiday packages.

Notice that the *Guardian's* interactions with customers served to make readers more engaged with the newspaper, but Porter and her team didn't stop there. In today's Internet world where social media has become essential to almost all businesses, the goal is not to rack up likes on Facebook or get the most clicks on a website. You engage your customers so that you can find out about them. As Brian Solis, the principal analyst at Altimeter, has said, "Sharing without analytics is essentially useless . . . engagement is not as valuable as insight, and . . . seeing things in context is more important than being popular."[61] Social media *does* engage consumers, but it is also an infinitely rich source of data you can use to create an accurate picture of your customers and what they want. As Joe Rospars, CEO of Blue State Digital, has put it, "Data is about having an understanding of what your relationship is with the people who are most important to you and an awareness of the potential in that relationship."[62]

CREATING A UNIFIED VISION

Like humans, a cuttlefish has two eyes it uses together to create a unified image of the world in what scientists refer to as binocular vision. This two-in-one perspective is what gives cuttlefish (and humans) depth perception. It's the reason why cuttlefish can accurately identify, pursue, and grasp prey. The cuttlefish marketer requires a similar unified vision.

The challenge for Guardian, as a media business, was to use data to merge its editorial side with its commercial side so they functioned seamlessly. If your business makes widgets, then your challenge as a cuttlefish marketer may look slightly different, but it will be based on the same principle, allowing you to use data to unite widget development and widget sales. If your company sells services of one sort or another, then data will allow you to create a unified binocular vision for developing and marketing those services

Trident Marketing, for example, provides direct-response marketing and sales services to leading brands that include DirectTV, ADT, and Travel Resorts of America. To do this, Trident handles more than four million calls a year for its clients. Steve Baldelli, the CEO at Trident Marketing, has used data analytics to drive the company's efficiency and growth, achieving some amazing results: over four years, the company's revenues increased by more than 1,000 percent, from $5 million to $53 million.[63] Using advanced database analytics,

Trident is now able to more precisely target customers through both digital and traditional promotions, combining data from external sources, such as credit bureaus, with data flowing from the company's telephone, customer-relationship reports, and order-entry systems. Trident also downloads clickstream data from Google and Bing every fifteen minutes. By applying predictive analytics to the constant incoming stream of data, Trident can create an incredibly detailed and broad-based view of sales trends. With near-instantaneous feedback, the company can then adjust its services accordingly, twisting and turning with true cuttlefish agility.

> *"Predictive analytics gave us a new dimension of thinking. Instead of seeing the business in two or three dimensions, we can effectively analyze hundreds of dimensions."*
>
> —Steve Baldelli, CEO, Trident Marketing[64]

DATA AND AGILITY

As Trident Marketing was able to do, Guardian News and Media could also do a number of things very quickly in response to data: develop new services and products; expand its subscription and membership business; relaunch an e-commerce site that had been languishing; and raise advertising revenues—and the company was able to rapidly fine-tune all of these ventures in response to readers' input. Well-utilized data is essential to this kind of agility.

Teradata Applications, a marketing software company, has also proved this. Lisa Arthur, the former CMO, said her company used data in order to rapidly develop and execute micro-campaigns that interact directly with customers. "We know from our data that third-party reports can be some of the best information to produce a follow-on conversation," she said, adding that "shortening time to insight has been really critical. How quickly can you synthesize data and take action on it?"[65]

Guardian News and Media, Trident, and Teradata are all good examples of companies that are using the cuttlefish marketing approach. They demonstrate how data can be organically linked to the overall business's agility.

THESE FIVE COMPANIES ARE PROVING THAT DATA EMPOWERS BOTH MARKETING AND PRODUCT DEVELOPMENT, WHILE SIMULTANEOUSLY IMPROVING CUSTOMER EXPERIENCE.

eBay's data-driven homepage, "the Feed," allows consumers to "follow" categories of items—from antiques to fashion accessories to car parts—and stay on top of the newest listings, while giving eBay an ongoing picture of what consumers want.

CMO Beth Comstock is using a customer hub of data visualization to reveal information such as how much energy certain appliances use and how much it costs. Comstock says that it's also her job as a marketer to find value in and make sense of the vast data sets available. She adds, "I get breathlessly excited about data."[66]

NETFLIX

Netflix has an algorithm that drives movie recommendations and continues to turn customer actions into a better experience, most recently with real-time processing. Netflix data usage is so successful that it comprises more than one-third of North America's Internet data consumption.[67]

Walmart ›‹

The autumn of 2011 was a turning point for Wal-Mart when it decided to upgrade its e-commerce by launching the social-, mobile-, and retail-focused @WalmartLabs, which uses semantic search algorithms to boost sales by understanding what customers search for. The lab's Social Genome Product also sorts through millions of social media posts to detect purchase intent and drive e-commerce.[68]

FINANCIAL TIMES

The *Financial Times* has a data team of more than thirty people, spread across three groups: data analytics and campaigns, data product development, and data technology. Together, they use audience data to increase the publication's circulation and to make the paper's advertising more competitive. They also map patterns in customer behavior to help convert readers to full-time subscribers.

ACTIVATING DATA

More than a century ago, the great advertising pioneer John Wanamaker said, "Half the money I spend on advertising is wasted; the trouble is I don't know which half."

That's not true today. As a marketing executive, you can track the performance of pretty much everything you do. But data alone won't give you the information you must have. You need to be able to *activate* data, using it effectively and efficiently to empower marketing.

Julia Porter is a phenomenal cuttlefish marketer who turned Guardian News and Media into a successful brand. Let's say, though, that the team at Guardian had figured out how to collect detailed data about their newspaper readers, but they didn't know what to do with this collection. They let it just sit there in big piles that kept getting bigger and bigger, doing no one the least bit of good. The sheer size of the data heaps would soon become overwhelming. The lower layers would rapidly cease to have any relevance, of course, but for the purposes of this story, we'll say Guardian didn't realize that. Data, instead of making the company agile and responsive, soon became a burden that weighed down everything in the business as people tried to sort through the enormous mass of information. Obviously, this is *not* what Guardian did, but if it *had*, it would have made as much sense as a cuttlefish that saw every detail of its prey, including size, shape, and tiniest movements, but just floated in the water, doing nothing. Not only would that cuttlefish not catch its prey but it would soon become some other predator's meal.

> *"Marketers today need to do more than just collect and analyze data. They need to be clear as to how the availability of this data will impact their marketing strategies and initiatives."*
>
> —Linda Popky, Founder and President, Leverage2Market Associates[69]

Or let's say that Trident spent millions of dollars collecting detailed data on the educational demographics of its customers. Now it's possible this information might have helped Trident understand its customers better, but it was not likely to have been the sort of dynamic input Steve Baldalli needed to keep a close eye on sales trends. Or imagine that Lisa Arthur (formerly at Teradata) had spent time, every day, analyzing the weather statistics in the cities where her customers did business. Again, sometimes seemingly unrelated data can give new perspectives, but in this case, it's doubtful that Teradata can use weather information to create the micro-campaigns that Arthur found so effective.

Focusing on the *wrong* data is nearly as bad as having no data. It would be like a cuttlefish that spent its time looking at above-water rock formations that have no bearing on its ability to detect and capture underwater prey. Sadly, these seemingly nonsensical situations are where some marketing departments find themselves. Everyone knows we have more data at our disposal than ever before. But activating that data—actually deriving meaningful insights from them and converting them into action—is easier said than done.

One of the most important factors for using data to empower marketing is to be able to define specifically what your goal is. In today's world, data is a vast haystack, and if you're going to look for a needle in that haystack, it helps a whole lot if you know what the needle looks like. Otherwise, you'll end up with a lot of useless needles that will do you absolutely no good. The job of a marketing executive is to define marketing goals precisely so IT teammates know what type of needle that marketing executive is looking for.

Let's say you're a publisher with a popular blog. Tracking how many people read your daily blog is great, but it's not as important as knowing how many of those readers then go to your catalog page and click the "buy" button. There are all kinds of tools to track just about everything, but ultimately what you want to determine are the things you're doing that lead to sales.

As James Dyson knows, the hypergrowth business requires finely tuned monitoring tools that are matched up with all the factors that affect its market. The necessary information has to be carefully defined and accurately collected, and systems have to be in place to allow the information to be applied nearly instantly to decision making. Ultimately, data is what triggers marketing sprints, product development, and customer relationships, as well as all the other strategies and processes that contribute to hypergrowth.

"I never guess. It is a capital mistake to theorize before one has data. Insensibly one begins to twist facts to suit theories, instead of theories to suit facts."

—Sherlock Holmes (Sir Arthur Conan Doyle)

ONGOING DATA

Data collection is not an extra activity that will make your marketing better. Rather, it's as essential to your company's existence as breathing is essential to your personal existence. And as respiration is constant and ongoing, so is the process of data collection. It's not something you can do once and be done with it. You can't even do it once every quarter or once every month.

To look at it another way, forget about cuttlefish vision for a moment, and think about your own—and it's instantly apparent how silly it would be if you were to use your eyes once every few weeks and then shut them again and see how far you could get with your eyes closed until you opened them again at some point in the future. For those of us who have our vision, seeing is inextricably linked with how we navigate our lives. When it comes to running a marketing department, we should look at data collection the same way.

We also need to keep in mind that data is fluid. It doesn't ever give you a final answer. Because the world is constantly changing at an ever-increasing pace, data changes as well. This requires an outlook that is far more flexible than what we may have been accustomed to in the past. As new information comes in, even our approach to data collection will constantly evolve.

Vince Campisi, the CIO at GE Software, describes the process like this:

> We may go after a particular outcome and try and organize a data set to accomplish that outcome. Once you do that, people start to bring other sources of data and other things that they want to connect. And it really takes you in a place where you go after a next outcome that you didn't anticipate going after before. You have to be willing to be a little agile and fluid in how you think about things. But if you start with one

outcome and deliver it, you'll be surprised as to where it takes you next.[70]

Julia Porter has explained that at Guardian, her team had to embrace an "always-on" way of doing marketing that relies on constant testing and learning, which in turn leads to *more* testing and more learning, in a never-ending cycle. "If you have a bucket of data, then use the technology to help you target better," Porter said. "It is all about fine-tuning your service and your offer so you get a better response to your marketing and then you get greater profitability further down the line."[71]

Here are some of the ways that data is empowering marketing in the twenty-first century:[72]

O Forty-four percent of business-to-customer marketers are using data and analytics to improve responsiveness.

O Forty-eight percent of sales and marketing departments use customer analytics, supporting the four key strategies of increasing customer acquisition, reducing customer churn, increasing revenue per customer, and improving existing products.

O It's now possible to embed intelligence into contextual marketing. Data analytics provides the foundation for creating scalable systems of insight to help alleviate this problem.

O Forrester found that data analytics increases marketers' ability to get beyond campaign execution and focus on how to make customer relationships more successful, leading to greater customer loyalty and improving customer lifetime.

o   Fifty-eight percent of Chief Marketing Officers say search engine optimization (SEO) and marketing, e-mail marketing, and mobile is where data is having the largest impact on their marketing programs today.

"The end has come for making marketing decisions based on gut instincts; everything marketers do in the digital world can now be tracked, from the first click all the way to the deal close. CMOs who do not embrace and accept this concept will likely not be CMOs for very long."

—Kurt Andersen, EVP Marketing and Sales Enablement, Savo[73]

TRANSPARENCY AND ACCOUNTABILITY

So, getting back to cuttlefish . . . imagine a cuttlefish that's really, really good at doing its jet-propulsion maneuver, zipping like lightning through the ocean depths in pursuit of the fish it loves to eat. It's been doing this maneuver for years, and it's great at jet propulsion, a cuttlefish superstar. Now let's pretend that the cuttlefish's eyes take in light data that tell it those quick little fish it's been eating all these years have disappeared from its neck of the sea. Meanwhile, it's seeing a whole lot of crabs. Cuttlefish that eat crabs survive quite nicely, but catching crabs requires a completely different sort of approach. Jet propulsion isn't all that useful for capturing something that skitters rapidly across the ocean floor first in one direction and then another.

Instead, the cuttlefish will have to use its ruffle-like fin to reverse its course just as fast as the crabs do.

But what if the cuttlefish says, "Jet propulsion has always worked for me in the past, so why shouldn't it work now?" despite the fact that its amazing vision clearly perceives that every time it does its jet-propelling thing, it overshoots, and the crab gets away. Or even worse, what if the cuttlefish says to itself, "I don't want to eat crab. I'm going to keep going after fish, even though I just don't see any around. If I keep doing what I've always done, though, I'm bound to find some fish."

All right, I know this is getting silly. But as marketers, we're prone to making the same mistake as our imaginary cuttlefish friend. We may understand that we must activate data, and in theory, we're good with that until the data tells us something we don't want to hear. Maybe we have a gut feeling we trust more than the data. Or maybe, without realizing it, we're so committed to a particular course of action we only use the data that supports our bias, and we overlook anything that would give us a more accurate picture of reality. We make the data say what we want it to say.

When we *really* activate data, however, it allows us to create a culture of transparency and accountability to objective facts.

When we *really* activate data, however, it allows us to create a culture of transparency and accountability to objective facts. At Guardian, Porter initially built her data-collection system in a way that made it transparent to the company's newspaper readers on what it was hoping to achieve, and that transparency became a built-in feature of Porter's approach. Data not only allowed the newspaper to pinpoint its readership groups for both targeted marketing and targeted offerings but also enabled the company to objectively assess the success of all its new efforts. Things that didn't work weren't hidden and continued. Transparency and accountability kept that from happening because everyone could clearly see what was working. Unique click-throughs on e-mails, for example, increased by 50 percent, and revenues from e-mail marketing went up by 100 percent. Sales went up by 60 percent, unique purchases increased by over 130 percent, and the mobile conversion rate rose by 137 percent. Meanwhile, RFM value (recency, frequency, and monetary value) analysis allowed the company to match the meaning of these numbers with detailed customer information.[74]

Creating a corporate culture of accountability and transparency means that *everybody*, not just the top-level executives, uses data. A culture like this makes sure the entire organism has access to information by distributing reports and talking about them, regardless of whether the results of a particular campaign, product, or service are positive or negative. After all, the cuttlefish doesn't use its vision to only locate and capture prey but also to avoid predators that might eat it. As human beings, we sometimes take a head-in-the-sand approach when we feel threatened by negative data, rather than understanding that negative data is actually just as useful as positive data.

"One approach [to transparency] is to develop a scorecard that tracks project progress and identifies breakdowns. Addressing these issues

cannot be about assigning blame; that would quickly create a toxic work environment. It should be about having clear accountability and working collectively to fix any problems."

—Matt Ariker, Martin Harrysson, and Jesko Perrey, McKinsey's Consumer Marketing Analytics Center[75]

A good example of negative data being essential to marketing is a direct-mail campaign. Most of us drop mail in blocks so we don't flood our call centers, and as the first waves of calls come in, we start to project the preliminary response rate. Negative data can tell us pretty quickly if a campaign (or a cell from our direct mail matrix) isn't working. And yet I've heard people say, "Let's just keep going. Maybe if we get more numbers, the response curve will improve."

Unfortunately, that doesn't usually happen. Negative data doesn't often miraculously shift directions. But there's a sunk-cost mentality that can lead you astray. You tell yourself to continue mailing out the rest of the direct mail because you've already spent a lot of time and money, and even though you haven't mailed all the pieces yet, you've already created and printed them. That's pretty much like a cuttlefish saying, "Gee, I swam all this distance to catch me some fish. Now that I'm here, I don't actually see any fish, but I'm just going to hang out for a while, hoping some will show up, so that I won't have made the trip for nothing."

Sunk-cost thinking seems to make sense at one level, but it leads to your wasting more time and more money. If the data tells you something is not working, cut your losses and switch as soon as possible to something that will work or to something you already know is working, based on results data. Negative data allows you to learn fast—and act fast.

In marketing, as in a hypergrowth business, you have to expect some things won't work. James Dyson, for example, created 5,126 vacuum cleaners that failed before he made one that worked.[76] If he had gotten tired of trying new things and gone with the 5,125th version, he would never have been able to create the successful business he did. By the same token, if he'd kept tinkering for years with that first version, determined to make it work, he never would have been able to move on to what *did* work.

When the data tells you that you've hit a wall, don't stay there and keep pounding your head against it. Go in another direction. Try something new.

"You never change things by fighting the existing reality. To change something, build a new model that makes the existing model obsolete."

—Buckminster Fuller

REDEFINING SUCCESS

Sometimes when I tell new clients that MSIGHTS will allow their team to have complete insight into all aspects of what's working and what's not working, I can see them cringe a little. I know what they're thinking: *I don't want that kind of transparency where you can see every wart and blemish.*

When I said something like this to Ed McLoughlin, though, he totally got it. "If something is not performing well," he said, "then I define success as meaning that I found out what wasn't working—and then we changed it. That to me is the success story." Ed now leads the global media and data sciences team at HP, Inc., and I'm convinced that his attitude toward failure has driven his incredible success over his career on the agency side and client side.

Success doesn't mean you get everything right the first time out of the gate. The *real* success story is embracing negative data and then jumping on them to turn around the things that aren't working. That's not to say that we *try* to fail. The goal of properly activated data is to help us succeed the first time as often as we can. But when we do fail, we should not let that discourage us. We also don't need to point fingers and place blame on the people responsible for what's not working.

A culture of transparency and accountability means that we discuss failure openly. At team meetings, we ask questions such as these:

- O   What things didn't work?

- O   Why didn't they work?

- O   How quick were you able to jump on it to improve it and what did you find out?

Good marketing leadership means we create an environment that allows for failure and uses it as an opportunity to build even greater success.

"You never learn from success, but you do learn from failure. . . . I got to a place I never could have imagined because I learned what worked and didn't work. We have to embrace failure and almost get a kick out of it. Not in a perverse way, but in a problem-solving way. Life is a mountain of solvable problems and I enjoy that."

—James Dyson[77]

DATA VERSUS CREATIVITY?

In 2013 the mobile phone network Three ran an ad for its 4G Internet service that rivaled the Old Spice Guy for sheer silliness. The ad, created by Wieden+Kennedy, features a Shetland pony dancing across the cliffs to a song by Fleetwood Mac. If you've seen the YouTube video (which went viral with more than six million views), you'd probably think the dancing pony was the brainchild of a zany group of marketers or an agency creative team.

Well, yes—but also no. Three's director of brand, Margaret Burke, said that data was at the heart of the Dancing Pony campaign.[78] The company used Internet usage data and subsequent market research to draw up the creative brief it gave to Wieden+Kennedy. Research conducted by BrainJuicer and commissioned by Three had found that the company's target audience loved sharing with friends various videos and photos—particularly of animals in funny situations—via their smartphones.[79] So this was the direction Three decided to take: a cute animal doing something funny. How about a dancing pony? What could be cuter and funnier than that?

The first step was to release a promotional video on video-sharing sites. The video also contained a link to a website where users could then create their own ads by choosing different sounds and moves. They then forwarded these ads to their friends or shared them, using social networks. The ad was supported by a web-based app hosted on YouTube. The app, which was called ponymixer.com, encouraged users to mix up the ad with different songs and animals and share their mixes with friends, with the best customizations featured in additional marketing activity. The people at Three were astonished by the results. More than six million viewers participated in the first two weeks, and more than a million Dancing Pony clips were created.

Three knew it had the data to launch a new spokesperson for its brand.[80]

Burke admitted that the Dancing Pony campaign couldn't have come into existence without the creative spark of the agency setting fire to the data insights, but she added, "I don't believe that you get that [creative spark] unless you're really clear about what you're trying to do. You only get the work that you set out to get."[81] She further explained that "rather than just play back the crazy things online that we all like to share, we wanted to actually contribute to it. We wanted to celebrate the seemingly silly stuff and also provide the means for people to mess with it and create their own little pieces of joy that they can share."[82]

The creative team just needed to come up with a blockbuster idea and then make a good pitch to the company's decision maker. That person's reaction was what made or lost the deal, regardless of how consumers ultimately responded to the campaign. Today's marketers have to answer to data rather than any single person's reaction to their clever ideas. This can give the impression that creativity no longer matters.

The Dancing Pony campaign proves that it does matter. But it also proves that creativity is most effective when it's held accountable to data. The *good idea* is no longer a subjective evaluation. Today we have to objectify creativity. Our job is no longer just the art of marketing. Instead, it's also the science of marketing. We have to line up our ideas with whatever really works.

But it's a balancing act. We still require that creative spark.

> *"Data is only as good as the meaning we create from it. We humans orchestrate all available data in innovative ways to create desirable customer experiences and business outcomes. The digital business landscape presents a canvas of sorts for people to be truly creative."*

—Blaine Mathieu, CMO, GoodData[83]

CHICKEN OR THE EGG?

In old-style marketing, the creative idea drove the entire process. Today things are more complicated because the data point is equally as important as the creative idea. A lot of creative ideas are driven by the data point, which helps orient and steer the ideas. On the other hand, generating the data point requires a creative idea in the first place. Otherwise, you wouldn't have any action in the market from which to *get* a data point. It's a chicken-or-the-egg situation. You can't pull apart creative ideas and data points. You can't say that one drives the other any more than you can say whether it's the chicken or the egg that came first.

So when people ask me, "Do you go with your gut and then use the data to check it? Or do you look at data and then go with your gut?" I always just say yes because it's a lot like that circle we talked about in the previous chapter, where technology shapes strategy and strategy contributes to technology. In a similar way, data will influence creativity, but creativity will give life to the data.

John Snyder, the CEO of Grapeshot, says that data-driven marketing will, in fact, "spark a creative rebirth." He goes on to say:

Back in the pre-programmatic days going all the way back to the dawn of advertising, creatives have used incomplete, sometimes even vague, notions of who their target audiences were to craft campaigns aimed to inspire, engage and ultimately incite purchase. Imagine how much fun they'll have and how much more successful they will be when their storytelling genius can be activated and informed by precise behavioral and demographic knowledge. We now can apply data to pinpoint the actual moment that people are auto shopping and serve them relevant and compelling messages about model features and financing options . . . We need to start promoting the truth, which is that data and technology will allow [creatives] to continue to flourish but with an updated toolkit.[84]

Ash Bendelow, the managing director of Brave, would agree. "Data should be a huge tool in the ongoing fight against mediocrity. Data should be the way in which agencies can remove subjectivity from decision making. Data should be embraced to help clients de-risk bravery when it comes to creativity. Data should enable greater creativity by giving clients confidence when buying braver ideas."[85]

And that's where you come in as the marketing director: you have to claim ownership of both sides—both creativity and data—in order to build the big-picture perspective. These are exciting days to be in marketing. Your job is to steer your departments through the heady opportunities and daunting challenges. To do that, you must own your data so you can lead and direct objective creativity.

OWNING YOUR DATA

Data feedback can be subtle, and you want full access to that subtlety. If you rely on an outside partner to manage and report your data, you may lose some of the details that could prove to be essential to your agility and success. Also, you should keep in mind that it's human nature for us to want to make ourselves look good, which means if you rely on an agency partner to report the data on its own efforts, you may be seeing through what might be an agency's rose-tinted glasses rather than getting an objective picture of the good, the bad, and the ugly.

Remember numbers can be massaged to reflect a particular bias, whether on purpose or by accident. Creating a narrative out of data can also be misleading because when data is given to you in story form, it may have been shaped to lead you in a particular direction. After all, even the best agencies in the world will feel pressure to deliver the great results you are looking for and that can cause an unintentional bias to shape the story in their favor. Even a slight bias will color what the net takeaway will be for you.

Numbers can be misleading in other ways as well. Take the concept of averages, for example. Say you read a report stating that the average open rate of your monthly e-blasts is 10 percent. That sounds like a successful e-blast campaign. Keep in mind, though, that if you were to put your feet in a campfire while your head was in a snow bank, your average body temperature could be normal, but you wouldn't be a very happy camper. If you're sending out thirty e-blasts a month, that 10 percent open rate might indicate that you had one e-blast that was incredibly successful—and twenty-nine duds.

By giving you all these cautionary tales about data, I'm not saying that agencies—and I have worked with and for some awesome ad/media agencies—can't be useful to you. They absolutely can be. Just be sure that you own the data in the same way that you own your technology. You want to be the one who directs the big-picture perspective, and you want to decide what the takeaway is when all's said and done.

The 2016 CMO Summit Survey asked CMOs what skills they felt were most necessary in today's marketing arena. The most common answers were digital marketing and data analytics. They also said that these skills were some of the most difficult to find.[86]

Part of owning your data means that you also carefully manage how data is dispersed within your organization. Sometimes when the same reports go out every week, looking exactly the same, structured into the same columns and graphs, people become too comfortable with glancing at them quickly. Because the reports don't always vary that much from week to week, a level of accidental complacency can develop. We don't feel the necessity to interpret the numbers from a fresh perspective.

I'm not saying that we don't need standard monitoring-type reports that are issued with a regular, predictable cadence. But as cuttlefish marketers, we have to push our teams to look at data in a less linear way and, instead, analyze from many different angles. We don't want our team just reading a bunch of numbers, week after week.

If everybody in the organization has access to the same information you do, weekly readouts will become obsolete because they should be replaced by discussion. After all, the only reason to do a readout is if you have access to something other people don't. I understand that some marketing executives may feel uncomfortable with this level of transparency. But readouts are another way to massage the numbers into telling a specific story. It may be a narrative that you've fallen in love with, and you want everyone else to love it as much as you do, but at that point, what you *really* need is additional perspectives from people who are more objective than you are. Owning the data doesn't mean that you get to shape them to suit yourself.

But it does mean that you face the challenge of linking together a wide variety of data sets in order to paint for your company a complete picture of the customer. Your job is to facilitate putting all the data pieces together. And then your next challenge is to turn a coherent customer data picture into a source of new value, using behavioral segmenting to understand which subgroups within your customer base will respond best to which media and message. And finally, you'll have to understand predictive analytics, which involves deciding which portfolio of products you should emphasize to different groups of customers.

If you were to look into a cuttlefish's eyes, you'd see that it has W-shaped pupils. These allow it to take in a wide panorama of visual information, and in a similar way, as marketing executives, we want data that gives us a 360-degree perspective. We get this by educating our teams to interact with data, not just to have data spoon-fed to them in a report or readout. Everyone in the organization should understand data and use it well. That attitude should be so embedded in the corporate mind-set that it contributes to the overall culture of transparency and accountability.

> *"In order to create sustained value and relevance [marketers] need to transform to become data experts. Suffice it to say, [they] are now in the tech business whether they like it or not. . . . Marketers need to seriously invest in owning more of the technology and data stack themselves."*
>
> —Brian Ferrario, VP Marketing, Drawbridge[87]

THE DATA TRIANGLE

When it comes to owning your data, imagine the three angles of a triangle. Each angle accounts for a portion of your time.

The first angle—one-third of your time—should focus on monitoring and tracking the traditional data, such as revenue versus expenses, net income, and so on. Think of those things as the basic things your doctor monitors when you go in for a physical—your heartbeat, your blood pressure—rather than any advanced diagnostic medical tests. If you're running your department as a hypergrowth business, you want to take advantage of the amazing array of sophisticated data that is out there, but you also want to keep track of your company's fundamental health (and how marketing is contributing to it).

The second angle of the data triangle consists of the vast array of results data that tells you what you're doing well. One-third of your time should focus on the things that the data confirms are working, understanding *why* they're working, and extrapolating that out to taking action.

The final angle of the triangle hinges on the things that the data indicates *aren't* working well. This last third of your time should be spent looking at why these things aren't working and what you can do to improve them.

If you keep this triangle in mind when you think about the way in which data rules your life as a marketing executive, it will help you balance your time and energy. You don't want to obsess over the basic financial data, and nor do you want to become so preoccupied with what you're doing wrong that you can't build on all the things you're doing right. The reverse of that is true as well: you don't want to be so excited about the things that are working perfectly that you forget to give any attention to the data that indicates what's not working.

Basic Financial Data

What's
Working

What
Isn't
Working

The Data Triangle

> *"These days, marketers know that the 'M' in CMO stands just as much for metrics as it does marketing."*

—Jess Nussbaum, Global Alliances & Partnerships, Dun & Bradstreet[88]

THE CONFIDENT MARKETER

I think of today's super successful marketers as being a lot like a basketball superstar whose team is playing the fifth game in the NBA finals with five seconds left in the game. His team is down by one, and he still has the grit and confidence to tell his coach, "Put me in. I want the ball," knowing that how he shoots will determine whether his team wins or loses the championship. The cuttlefish marketing executive has that same kind of confidence.

And it's not misplaced confidence. Just as a cuttlefish can trust the sophisticated visual information its eyes deliver, you too have so much data available to you that there's no reason why you shouldn't have phenomenal information always at your fingertips. If you're activating that data, maintaining accountability and transparency, you can and should feel confident in your own success. You can learn fast—and move fast. Most of all, you won't have to outsource your leadership, which means you can be an active player in your own success.

"Confidence and empowerment are cousins in my opinion. Empowerment comes from within and typically it's stemmed and fostered by self-assurance."

—Amy Jo Martin, CEO of Digital Royalty

TECHNOLOGIST'S PERSPECTIVE

IVAN AGUILAR, CO-FOUNDER OF MSIGHTS

Sometimes it is said that technology has no feelings when it comes to numbers. For those of us who are technologists, a number is a number. We don't attach sentimental value to it, so we present the facts as they are. While working with MSIGHTS, we've learned to display the facts but also provide context and meaning, such as understanding if the number represents a high cost per acquisition or a low acquisition rate. This sensibility is created through alerts that are configured in the system and through the daily processing of the data. We need to provide the facts and all the supporting numbers, so when the marketing team members read them, they can provide a story based on the context and the facts. The marketing team depends on information provided by technology, so it is very important to show what's in the facts, meaning, what sources are loaded, what data points are missing, and so on.

KEY POINTS TO REMEMBER

→ Data is what empowers you and your department, giving you the information you require to be flexible and fast.

→ Activating data means choosing the right data to pay attention to and then taking appropriate action based on that information.

→ Define your end goals in order to use the right data effectively.

→ Data is fluid, which means that activating it is an ongoing, continuous process.

→ Data is what allows you to be transparent and accountable to what really works.

→ We must redefine success to mean activating both negative and positive data so that we learn fast what works and what doesn't.

→ Data and creativity need to work together, each driving the other.

→ Own your data by being the one who directs its collection, dispersal, application, and internal and external usage.

→ Use the data triangle—one angle represents traditional, basic financial data; another represents data that indicates what's working; and the third angle represents data that tells you what's not working—to keep your attention and balance to data.

→ Use data to give you confidence in your ability to lead your department.

CHAPTER 5

TRAIT #4: DON'T OUTSOURCE YOUR LEADERSHIP

BE AN ACTIVE PLAYER IN YOUR OWN SUCCESS

The cuttlefish brain has several parts, as the human brain does, each responsible for various functions. One lobe controls the animal's tentacles, for example, while another oversees breathing, and yet another is responsible for the camouflage changes in its skin. All these functions are routinely carried out by each of the appropriate lobes of the brain. Unlike humans, however, cuttlefish have additional brain lobes that are outside the brain casing. These are the optic lobes, which are capable of doing far more than merely controlling the creature's vision. Stimulus of the optic lobes can trigger all the behaviors and actions normally controlled by the other parts of the brain. This is one reason why the cuttlefish can be so phenomenally sensitive to its environment: its brain structure gives it the ability to respond instantly to light data as it's received from the eyes, sending out messages throughout the cuttlefish's entire nervous system.[89]

So how do we carry the analogy over into marketing? Well, I think the lesson we can learn from the cuttlefish's unique brain function is this: as the marketing executive, you should not outsource your thinking. This doesn't mean you have to micromanage your team, and it doesn't mean that you can't leverage agency partners and outside consultants. All members of your team should be as capable of independent thought and function as the cuttlefish's brain lobes are. But when it comes down to what makes you successful, you don't want to sit back waiting for everyone else to take care of things. You want to be the one in charge.

I know you already have a lot to be responsible for—I know, I've been in your shoes. It's tempting to let your agency partner handle the things we've been talking about so far—being agile, using technology, and analyzing the data—while you focus on corporate alignment, stakeholder inclusion, and all of the other time-consuming internal operations. But relying on an agency partner to do all your thinking is simply not the fastest, most efficient way of doing things. It won't make you agile. Just the opposite, in fact.

Cuttlefish marketers take an active role in their own success. They make it happen. They don't outsource their leadership to outside partners.

TODAY'S MARKETING PARTNERSHIPS

In January 2015 the executives at the advertising and marketing holding company MDC Partners, and Salesforce.com, the cloud-computing company, began discussing how they might work together to use marketing technology. They realized, though, that they were missing the software that would make their collaboration work. "What we kept looking for," Michael Bassik, president of digital operations at MDC, recently said, "was an agency who really could bridge the tech and creativity gap." Eventually, they invested in the digital marketing agency Pierry. Pierry's software, working with Salesforce software, would help agencies interpret data to create, manage, and distribute more personalized content such as e-mails or mobile ads.[90]

The MDC–Salesforce–Pierry relationship isn't a unique one. Clearly, you *need* to form partnerships of one sort or another if you're going to survive in the modern marketing world. More and more marketing technology firms are working with agency groups in order to deliver data-based, individual-focused campaigns. "What Salesforce identified," Bassik said, "was that creative agencies were the best at producing content but hadn't focused on implementing technology solutions . . . When you control content, you get better insights into what's working."[91]

Other companies are finding different ways to achieve similar goals. IBM, for example, recently acquired a digital creative shop called Resource/Ammirati, with the goal of more effectively reaching IBM's marketing goals. According to Kelly Mooney, the CEO of Resource/Ammirati, "The CMO and CIO increasingly have to partner to tackle shared objectives."[92]

Mark Read, CEO of the digital agency Wunderman, said something very similar, "I don't think CMOs or CIOs make decisions independently." Read's agency entered a formal partnership with Marketo, a marketing automation company that can track customers' actions from the time they get an e-mail promotion to the online point of sale. This partnership will help Wunderman build more accurate profiles of what customers are doing, so it can send customized, targeted messages.[93]

A new Omnicom Group agency is dedicating itself exclusively to McDonald's, with four main themes central to its organization: the consolidation of marketing services across Omnicom agencies, access to data, breaking down silos within Omnicom and McDonald's, and transparency on both the agency and client sides of the business. The agency's goal is to work with McDonald's to revolutionize the company and its sales.[94]

What all these companies have in common is that they have found ways to merge the functions of what were once considered separate aspects of a company. Because today's advertising model is based on targeted, contextually relevant content, delivered to a global world that is increasingly dependent on personal devices, data is inextricably linked with marketing's creative process. That's a reality in today's world.

The response to this reality has been, as I mentioned in chapter 3, that the number of marketing technology (martech) vendors is growing exponentially. If you haven't already experienced for yourself how confusing this can be, a glance back at the image on page "Graphic courtesy of Scott Brinker" on page 67 will make it clear how many pieces there are to choose from in this particular puzzle. With one agency handling one thing, another something else, and yet another agency doing something else for a company, if there's no one who is responsible for the overall big picture, that picture soon becomes very fragmented.

The problem then is this: how can in-house marketing departments, agency partners, and martech companies marry creativity with tech capabilities in a way that makes sense in today's world? Modern marketing can't function without technology and data, but if your company isn't an IBM or an MDC or a McDonald's, you probably can't go out and partner up with your own exclusive agency to provide you with all the services necessary. You'll have to find other ways to outsource some aspects of your work. It makes sense to make use of all the resources out there to supplement your own.

What doesn't make sense, however, is trying to outsource your thinking and leadership as well. As we discussed in chapters 2 and 3, you, as the marketing executive, are the only one who sees the big-picture goals—the directions you have to take to be a hypergrowth business—so you should be the one who integrates everything else to reach those goals.

To do this, you'll need to think about your relationships with outside agency partners in a new way, as a new kind of partnership. Andrew Bruce, the CEO of Publicis Communications, recently said, "Partnerships between agencies and clients in which both entities are working toward shared objectives are key for the industry's future." According to Bruce, these partnerships allow the agency to "become a part of a client's world and ambitions."[95]

> *"Brand involvement doesn't die—it morphs to an overall planning, strategy and creative excellence role, all backed by results and data driven from a highly efficient and knowledgeable team and systems specializing in global media properties.... It is essential that brand marketers control their software stack driving their business by owning the contracts."*
>
> —Gary Milner[96]

OWNING THE BIG PICTURE

Lenovo digital marketer Gary Milner recently compared the transformation process in twenty-first-century marketing to the shift
experienced by US energy companies as environmental, governmen-
tal, and consumer factors combined to decrease coal consumption.
Major change doesn't usually happen by consensus, he pointed out;
it happens because of executive-level leadership.[97]

Let's take Milner's analogy a little further: alternative energy and
natural gas companies are a necessary component of the industry's
transformation, but left to themselves, their smaller and conflicting
perspectives would end up going nowhere. Someone has to direct
the big process, and the same is true in marketing. To go back to our
friend the cuttlefish, when the sea is teaming with both potential
prey and dangerous predators, the cuttlefish's ability to act instantly
from a centralized portion of its brain means that it doesn't respond
in contradictory and ineffectual ways, jet-propelling first in one
direction and then another, waving its tentacles at the same time
that it's camouflaging itself as a stone. As a marketing executive, you
too want all your responses to be coordinated, all working together
toward the same overall goals.

When there's no one who owns the entire big picture, it not
only hurts marketing but also costs the company unnecessary dollars.
Reinforcing my point that marketing departments have to be run as
hypergrowth businesses, in a recent media post, Milner asserted that
"CEOs of large corporations still have not realized that the common
global IT elements found in expense systems, HR systems, and
travel systems are increasingly possible with media buying. There is
no reason for all of the company to not use the same media-buying
systems, globally forming an IT stack for marketing."[98]

All elements of a business's cost chain—including both production and marketing—must be understood and optimized. As Milner pointed out, "There are still many people running significant brand budgets who don't understand the field they are playing in and are driven by reach and frequency metrics only. Do you really need the 1.4 billion campaign impressions in a 250 million population, when you are targeting a subsegment of this large population? Waste abounds."[99]

Waste is one of the major flaws of some of the huge, bloated agencies of the past. Their large staffs and big buildings made for massive overheads that drove expenses higher. They also wasted both time and money because they were so large and cumbersome that they couldn't be agile. Instead of turning on a dime, they lumbered along, slow to make decisions and slow to take action. Don't get me wrong. There were exceptions to the rule: large, nimble agencies that could revise their tactics quickly. You want to build partnerships with these exceptions or, more realistically, with highly specialized experts, rather than hand over your marketing to a giant, all-inclusive dinosaur that will gobble up money and time, delivering little in return.

GET WHAT YOU PAY FOR

When you try to outsource your thinking to outside vendors and agency partners, there are other types of waste that may be going on as well. According to *Advertising Age,* "Kickback payments tied to U.S. media-agency deals are real and on the rise,"[100] This means you can't be sure if your money is being effectively spent on your behalf.

Kickback arrangements come in a variety of shapes and colors. In some cases, a media agency might request that several hundred thousand dollars of a company's million-dollar ad funds be directed to pay for presentations handled by an affiliate agency. The presentations are actually worth just a fraction of the money being passed along to pay for them. According to one anonymous adtech executive, "It's positioned as if this affiliate is going to do 'media planning' or 'media optimization,' but they do nothing and one never hears from them again. They just receive the check."[101]

Media agencies publicly deny that this sort of thing is going on, but according to industry executives who spoke privately with *Advertising Age*, "U.S.-based marketers are being kept out of the loop about billions of dollars that agencies make back from deals on clients' behalf, whether in the form of opaque markups, kickbacks, or undisclosed rebates. One agency executive estimates that undisclosed rebates account for about 5 percent of media-agency networks' total global revenue, while other ex-agency employees put the proportion higher."[102]

I've also seen smaller-budget marketing departments and companies get into problems when they start working with big agencies, hoping to benefit from a trickle-down network effect. They think that if they throw their smallish budget into a big agency that is already buying a billion dollars in media, they should theoretically get a better deal by piggybacking onto their relationship with media companies. In my years of experience with clients, however, I've rarely seen that better deal actually materialize. Agencies are assets at marketing executives' disposal, but when marketing executives work with them, they shouldn't assume they're getting something they're not.

PICKING THE BEST

When you're the central brain that directs the big picture, rather than outsourcing your thinking and leadership, you're in a position to sort through the agencies out there and form relationships with the ones that will offer you the most expertise for your specific marketing needs. Rather than hiring a single company to be your brain for you, you focus on matching the best partner with your individual needs.

Let's say you're in the middle of a campaign when a whole bunch of new opportunities suddenly opens up. Now you require mobile management and social media. If you're already in position to reach out to other agency partners with the right skill sets, you have more flexibility to react as the campaign unfolds.

One way this plays out most consistently is with tech vendors. Where once a single agency might have contracted out your marketing and ad tech for you, now it makes more sense for you, as the marketing director, to do that directly. You'll have more agility if an agency no longer manages your tech relationship for you.

Once upon a time, the big marketing deals were made with media outlets. Now, though, it's the data and the technology that enable the media and the message. When you hear about companies making deals with Google or Facebook, for example, what's happening is really a tech deal rather than a media deal. And they're direct deals. They don't go through any agency.

Remember your job is to keep all your guns pointing at your target, that big picture you're ultimately trying to reach. Your clarity of mind is what sorts through all the outside agencies and pulls together the right pieces for your big picture.

How do you do this? Well, for one thing, consider reviewing the agencies you already work with.

TAKE CONTROL OF THE RELATIONSHIP

Advertiser Perceptions recently reported that nearly two-thirds of leading US advertisers are planning for creative agency reviews in the next year, while nearly the same number will also be reviewing their partnerships with media and digital agencies.[103] More and more marketers are focused on thinking for themselves. They're no longer willing to outsource their thinking.

At the same time, though, you should have an effective working relationship with your outside partners. When it comes to any kind of relationship, whether between individuals or between organizations, trust is essential on both sides. In 2014 *USA Today* and the marketing agency RPA funded a study on the relationship between brands and their creative partners. The study, which involved about 150 senior-level agency and brand marketing leaders, found that 98 percent of both clients and agencies believe that a trust-based union leads to better work.[104] Unfortunately, the survey also found that there are many issues threatening this trust, including "disagreement about the role of creativity, different appetites for creative risk, a perceived lack of understanding of each other's business, and an absence of honest and open lines of communication." [105]

Here is a selection of survey results from "The Naked Truth," the study funded by *USA Today* and RPA:

O   Eighty-eight percent of marketing executives claim to speak their mind freely, even when it's uncomfortable. But among agency leaders who frequently interact with clients, the percentage that believes this is true is only 36 percent.

O   Almost two-thirds of both the marketers (60.5 percent) and agency executives (70 percent) surveyed admitted they don't share the same definition of creativity.

○ When asked how much even the best creative work could move their business, on average marketers said 26 percent, while agency executives said 48 percent.

○ Seventy-six percent of agency executives say their clients are afraid to take risks.

○ A majority of marketing executives (56 percent) say that their agencies are more interested in "selling" them their work rather than solving their problems.[106]

One of the essential ingredients of building the trust necessary for a healthy relationship is good communication. RPA's SVP of Creative, Marketing and Innovation, Tim Leake, has suggested that a primary "action step" to improve trust levels in the client-agency relationship is to "focus as much on interpersonal communication as we do mass communication."[107]

Clear communication is essential to the cuttlefish marketer.

CUTTLEFISH COMMUNICATION

At this point, you may think I'm stretching the cuttlefish analogy a bit. After all, how can a creature that's basically a giant head with a bunch of tentacles do much when it comes to communication? It has got a great brain, a fantastic nervous system, and phenomenal eyes, but how can it possibly communicate with other cuttlefish let alone with other life forms?

Well, as it turns out, cuttlefish use that phenomenal centralized brainpower of theirs to communicate quickly and diversely. Since they are so dependent on light data for navigating their world, it's not surprising that they also communicate visually, through four methodologies: skin coloration, skin texture, posture, and movements. You might think this would give them a pretty limited vocabulary, but actually, cuttlefish can combine as many as seventy-five chromatic (color-related) elements, seven textures, fourteen postures, and seven movements to convey a fairly sophisticated range of messages.[108]

And cuttlefish not only communicate different things but also adapt their style of communication for different situations. They can even adapt their communication styles for gender differences. For example, when female cuttlefish "talk" to each other—or when they look at themselves in the mirror—they take on a splotchy skin color, communicating quite differently from the way they do with males or with prey.[109] Male cuttlefish may give themselves a zebra pattern to warn away other males.[110] They can also carry on more than one conversation at once, using one side of their body to express their interest to females, while with the other side of their body they warn other males not to interrupt their romance.[111] Cuttlefish can even communicate deceptively: when a cuttlefish is hunting, for example, it might send dark, 3-D waves of color rippling over its body, saying to its prey, "Hey! Stop and watch me!"[112] The unspoken part of that message is, "So I can eat you!" Small males also avoid altercations with other males by "talking like a woman" with body splotches accompanied by specific tentacle movements.[113]

So, what does all this say to us as marketers? Well, what I see is that owning the relationship doesn't mean we keep our perspective all to ourselves. If that were the case, we'd be practicing old-style hierarchical management—just in a new way. We don't want to outsource our leadership and thinking, but we do want to be able to communicate clearly from our position of active involvement.

As the cuttlefish proves, communication can take place in all sorts of ways. You could talk to a cuttlefish until you were blue in the face without it comprehending one word you said, but you'd be wrong if you dismissed your tentacled friend as being incapable of communication. You may be making the same mistake with outside agencies that don't speak the same language you're accustomed to using. When working with agencies, you may have to adapt your style and even the form of communication. What works in one setting won't necessarily work in another. The cuttlefish marketer always adapts to new situations, rather than insisting on a static, status quo approach.

Unfortunately, the Advertiser Perceptions study found that there are major communication breakdowns in many client-agency relationships. While 88 percent of clients claim they speak their minds freely to their agency, only 36 percent of agency partners agree. On the other hand, 90 percent of agencies say they truly understand their clients' business, but only 65 percent of the clients agree. Obviously, the two sides must communicate better with each other, and as the marketing director, you must make sure that happens.[114]

The Advertiser Perceptions report made clear that problems with agency relationships aren't always the agencies' fault. Advertisers placed blame on themselves as well, with nearly half admitting that they didn't give agencies meaningful key performance indicators that could help them be successful; 40 percent said they didn't even share sales data with agencies.[115] If you're not communicating clearly with your outside partners, then both sides are reduced to the sort of interactions that would be typical of a bunch of half-blind cuttlefish. No wonder trust breaks down in situations like these. Without trust and clear communication, how can you possibly hope to make outside agencies a seamless part of your organic function?

It's easy to blame agency partners for all the things wrong with the relationship, but taking an active role in our success as marketing executives also means we accept the responsibility of making our partnership relationships work better. We must take the lead at building better communications that will foster trust and empower working relationships.

BUILDING TRUST WITH YOUR CUSTOMERS

Trust isn't only essential to effective relationships with outside partners; it's also essential to your relationship with your customers, and it's also something you can't outsource.

It used to be that your company gave you a budget, which allowed you to hand over much of your marketing and advertising to an agency, while your job was to approve or disapprove specific campaigns and media plans. Today's marketing, however, requires your active participation. In fact, the very nature of marketing pushes active involvement back into your court.

For example, today's consumers want to interact directly with your brand via social media. The author David Garland[116] reminds us to ask these questions before handing over social media marketing to an agency:

- What exactly is being offered and what should be offered?

- Can an agency assist with content creation?

- Can an agency find relevant articles/other content in your niche to share on Twitter, Facebook, and so on?

- Can an agency suggest people to follow?

- Can an agency set up a Facebook page and Twitter account for you?

- Can an agency suggest tweeting topics?

- ○ Can an agency post content to your Twitter and Facebook accounts?

- ○ Can an agency suggest blogs and forums you should be participating in/on?

The answers to these questions, says Garland, is a qualified yes, but he goes on to say that the more important questions are these:

- ○ Can an agency be you and act like you online?

- ○ Can an agency form relationships with people?

- ○ Can an agency employ small talk and make it look as if it is coming from your CEO?

The answer to these three questions, according to Garland, is a "resounding **no**." You can't ask your agency partners to pretend to be you and expect them to pull off the same level of customer engagement that you could. The digital world fosters genuine and immediate contact between brands and their users.

You can't outsource trust.

BE THE QUARTERBACK MORE THAN THE COACH

At this point, I'm going to set aside cuttlefish analogies for just a moment because American football offers another good way to understand the relationship you should have with your outside partners. Think of yourself as a quarterback playing out on the field, rather than the coach watching and directing from the sidelines.

Your company's SVP or CMO have roles more like a coach's. The coach has a lot of other things to manage beyond what's happening on the field, including personnel, working with the team's owner(s), press, and so on, but quarterbacks must be out there on the field, in the throes of the play as it evolves around them. They must be able to see what their options are, determine priorities in response to what's going on, and be able to do it on the fly. Doing that well is what builds trust in the rest of the team members (and even the fans).

There's a lot of pressure on the quarterback. When you're reacting that quickly to things, mistakes get made. A marketing director can be tempted to evade all that responsibility if something goes wrong. The safer route might be to outsource "quarterbacking" to an agency. That way, if an ad doesn't work or an entire campaign bombs, the marketing director can let the agency take the blame. It takes real strength and courage to be a quarterback in the game.

AGENCIES HAVE VALUE, BUT YOU'RE THE BRAIN

Please don't get me wrong. I am not anti-agency. Agencies and outside vendors such as consultants can, absolutely, provide value to you and your company. I've worked with great agency partners that had some very innovative ideas, so I know how much agencies can bring to the table.

But at the end of the day, as the marketing executive, you've got to make the call. You are the one who's on the field. You can't sit there and outsource your responsibility. You must be an active player in the game.

An organism needs its brain for all its body parts to work together as a whole. It also needs that brain to communicate clearly with the rest of the world. As marketing directors, we must be that brain, directing not only our agency partnerships but also our internal teams.

> *"To be a great quarterback, you have to have a great leadership, great attention to detail, and a relentless competitive nature."*
>
> —Russell Wilson, quarterback for the Seattle Seahawks

KEY POINTS TO REMEMBER

→ Effective partnerships empower modern marketing.

→ As a marketing executive, you must maintain your own thought leadership rather than outsourcing it to an outside agency.

→ Own the big picture; don't expect an agency to be responsible for overseeing the larger perspective.

→ Be careful to avoid agencies involved in unusual kickback arrangements that waste your dollars.

→ Build healthy relationships with your outside partners, based on trust and good communication.

→ Don't expect to be able to outsource customer trust.

→ Always be an active player in your success; be the quarterback, not the coach.

CHAPTER 6

TRAIT #5: BUILD A DIFFERENT KIND OF TEAM

BRING NEW SKILL SETS TO THE TABLE

Your average mollusk—say a clam or a snail—has three body parts: a brain, a foot, and what's known as a visceral mass, which contains the various tubes and valves that allow it to carry out circulation and digestion. A cuttlefish, however, is an immensely complicated organism. Its body parts aren't much like ours—or like any vertebrate's—but together, they make a remarkably agile and intelligent creature.

We've already described the cuttlefish's amazing skin, nervous system, eyes, and brain, but this peculiar creature also has many other unique features. Its multifunctional mantle cavity gives it jet-propulsion abilities while also aiding its respiration. Its fin, which looks like a fluttery ruffle circling its body, is a powerful muscle that allows the cuttlefish to maneuver in pretty much any direction—backward, forward, sideways, and even in circles—quickly and efficiently. Although the cuttlefish has no ears, it has lines along the outside of its body that contain tiny hair cells that are incredibly sensitive to the slightest wave in the sea. These microscopic hairs function so accurately that cuttlefish can both escape predators and hunt even in total darkness, detecting the presence of their prey by the tiniest of movements. Once it has its prey cornered, two long tentacles dart out from the cuttlefish's body to grab the prey, and the cuttlefish's eight arms grasp it tight.[117]

The cuttlefish is the oddest collection of peculiar individual features. Nothing like it exists anywhere in the vertebrate world. And yet the cuttlefish is a remarkably successful predator that has survived for eons. The fossil record indicates that ancestors of the cuttlefish have been around almost since the beginning of complex life forms 550 million years ago.[118] This bizarre creature may not look like your definition of a beautiful animal, but clearly, when it comes to being a predator, its strange collection of traits and strengths gets the job done.

When we put together our marketing team, that should be our goal as well: bringing together a group of individuals who can get the job done. To do that, we must be clear as to what the job actually is.

Old-style marketing directors would have said their job was to execute marketing campaigns. Today's marketing executives must define their job as generating orders or high-quality leads in the most efficient way, deploying every marketing dollar as efficiently as possible to drive their company's success. Notice that this definition of the marketing executive's objective crosses that great divide that once existed between marketing and sales. And that means we must bring a whole new set of skills to our teams.

The cuttlefish marketer is required to build a different kind of team from the old-style marketing team. Oh, we still need creative people to help come up with campaign ideas. But just as important, now, are the individuals who can help us accomplish all the things we've already discussed in this book. They include statisticians and other people who can analyze data, technicians, operations research, accountants, and people with whatever skill sets are necessary to drive our company's sales. Today's teams don't look like yesterday's.

> *"The strength of the team is each individual member. The strength of each member is the team."*
>
> —Phil Jackson, New York Knicks president and former Chicago Bulls coach

TWENTY-FIRST-CENTURY TEAM BUILDING

In 2002, Billy Beane, the general manager of Major League Baseball's Oakland A's, had the problem of how to win in the Major Leagues

with a budget that was smaller than that of nearly every other team. The conventional wisdom was that if you wanted to succeed in the Major Leagues, you built a team of big names and amazing hitters and pitchers, but that took lots of money. Beane and his staff decided to try another approach. They used sta-

Billy Beane

tistical data to find the players necessary to win. Beane was convinced that a winning team could be had by affordable methods if he were to use the numbers to find hitters with high on-base percentages and pitchers who got lots of ground-outs.

Beane defined the big objective for all winning teams: get people on base. Statistically, the more often you can get a man on base, the more often you score runs, and the more often you score runs, the more often you win. Ultimately, it doesn't really matter if players hit home runs or they get walked so long as they can score runs.

So, with the help of a Harvard-educated economist, Beane defied tradition, the media, the fans, and his own scouting department by looking for the cheapest players who got on base the most and building a team out of young, affordable players and inexpensive, cast-off veterans. These were players no one thought could win, a bunch of players with traits that seemed nearly as odd as a cuttlefish's grab-bag collection of body parts. But Beane's players proved everyone wrong. They turned the Oakland A's into a winning team.

Billy Beane defined success and team building in out-of-the-box ways, and he built a team with the skills he required to drive his core objective. His story, made famous by both the movie and the book *Moneyball* by Michael Lewis, has changed the way the world looks at team building.

In the movie *Moneyball*, when John Henry, the owner of the Red Sox, interviewed Billy Beane to bring him on as his general manager, Henry said something along these lines, "Any team that's not breaking down their organization and rebuilding it based on your method are dinosaurs, and they're going to be sitting on their butts, watching the Red Sox win the World Series." Beane was offered the job of GM of the Red Sox, but he turned it down and stayed with the A's. The Red Sox, however, put into practice Beane's data-based team-building principles. Two years later, the Red Sox won the World Series for the first time since 1918.

Beane proved that data is the key to a strong team. When it comes to your marketing team, well-activated data will also give you the information you require to choose people with the necessary skills. Successful marketing teams are no longer made up of a bunch of people with marketing degrees any more than winning baseball teams have to all be superstars. Instead, you want the wide range of skills that will make you agile in today's fast-paced market.

Billy Beane was clear at the outset about the key performance indicator he would use to judge players—on-base percentage—which made his decisions very clear when it came to selecting his team. If you use the same principles to build your marketing team—deciding up front the criteria by which you'll judge your marketing efforts—your decisions will also become clearer.

The founder and CTO of HubSpot, Dharmesh Shah, reminds us:

The startup world is filled with superstars that get overlooked or don't quite make it because they're "quirky" or otherwise don't fit preconceived patterns of [what] people think a person in a given role should look and feel like. None of that matters . . . Figure out what success looks like for a given role, and ignore the irrelevant details.[119]

"CMOs who surround themselves with people who can dig into ... data and translate it so creative thinkers can make strategic decisions based on data points are going to rise to the top."

—Hank Summy, partner, LiquidHub[120]

THE AGILE TEAM

When the power went out during the 2013 Super Bowl, Oreo's marketing team was already in place to take advantage of the moment in an unexpected way. The cookie company tweeted, "Power out? No problem. You can still dunk in the dark." The tweet was retweeted more than sixteen thousand times. Oreo's Twitter following increased by about eight thousand. On Facebook the post garnered nearly twenty thousand likes, and Oreo went from having two thousand Instagram followers to thirty-six thousand.[121]

"The tweet heard 'round the world" took lightning-fast advantage of a circumstance that no one could have predicted. It looks like the perfect example of agile marketing—and it is. But it would never have happened if Oreo hadn't already had a team in place with the skill set necessary to leap on the opportunity presented by the blackout.

According to Lisa Mann, senior vice president of cookies at Oreo's parent company, Kraft Foods, "The Super Bowl tweet made our social media outreach seem like an overnight success, but it took a year and a half of practice to prepare for that moment."[122] The team that made it happen, Mann said, was made up of marketing, legal, and tech staff who had learned to work together so smoothly that they were able to instantly capitalize on the blackout incident in real time.

Nearly two years earlier, as the company prepared for its hundredth birthday, marketing executives decided to launch a daily social media campaign. The company set up a war room where the team worked together to determine what was meaningful to its social media followers and how they could deliver it. By the time the lights went out during the Ravens versus the 49ers game, the team was a well-oiled machine that interacted live with social media every day.

The broad-based skills of the team members put Oreo in place to take advantage of whatever unfolded during the game (although they'd been thinking more along the lines of a mind-blowing play than a power outage). Statisticians and data analysts knew, for example, that 36 percent of Super Bowl viewers would be watching on a smaller screen than a TV, such as a smartphone. Once the big night arrived, Lisa Mann explained, the cookie company made sure to have on hand everyone they needed for an enormous real-time social-media push.[123] Oreo's team, that night, included copywriters, a strategist, and artists, all ready to react to any situation in ten minutes or less.[124]

That team is what allowed them to be so agile and interactive with their consumers. A similar kind of team is what also allowed the Old Spice Guy to be so successful. Iain Tait, the creative director at Wieden+Kennedy, said of the Old Spice Guy campaign, "One of the unique things taking place in the studio is we have a team of social media people, we have the Old Spice community manager, we have a social media strategist, a couple of technical people, and a producer. And . . . they're working in collaboration with the creative team that are there to pick out the messages that: 1. Have creative opportunity to produce amazing content; or 2. Have the ability to then embed themselves in an interesting or virally-relevant community . . . it's a really interesting combination."[125]

"We cannot have people with singular skills. And the way I build out my organization is I look for people with a major and a minor. You can major in analytics, but you can minor in marketing strategy. Because

if you don't have a minor, how are you going to communicate with other parts of the organization? Otherwise, the pure data scientist will not be able to talk to the database administrator, who will not be able to talk to the market-research person, who will not be able to talk to the email-channel owner, for example."

—Zoher Karu, vice president and chief data officer at eBay

WHAT TO LOOK FOR WHEN YOU'RE BUILDING YOUR TEAM

As you go through the process of selecting the members of your team, there's always a temptation to pick people who are a lot like you. When you sit down to talk with them, you connect. You feel comfortable with them. You speak the same language. You feel as though you could all work together smoothly and easily. Well, all that's fine and good. But do you really want a bunch of people just like you on your team?

For one thing, if you were to put together a team of mini-yous, you wouldn't have the diverse skill sets necessary for today's marketing world. And second, if you're like me, deep in your heart you're still an old-style marketer who's struggling to transform yourself into a cuttlefish marketer. So, odds are good that you feel most comfortable with people who are also old-style marketers. Those are the folks who talk the same language as you do. They are *not* the people you want on your new-style marketing team. You want a team of individuals who understand the new world of marketing, people who are agile, IT savvy, and data driven.

"The future is in the middle," according to Andy Roach, the CTO at CDS, an Omnicom Group company. Roach has described the shift he's experienced from chasing "English majors and marketing majors to chasing tech-savvy users." He wants "people who have used systems, who are comfortable learning SaaS tools, people who have used Marketo and Salesforce and HubSpot, people who understand how to diagnose or look through data from Google."[126]

It's not all that different from the challenge Billy Beane faced when he sat down to build a winning baseball team. Imagine Beane knowing he had to find twenty-five guys to make a baseball team but knowing nothing about the positions he'd be recruiting for. If he hadn't known he needed a first baseman, a second baseman, a shortstop, and so on, his job would have been a lot harder. As the marketing executive, you too must know the positions you must fill, and you must know the strengths that will allow individuals to perform well in those roles. Once you've clearly defined all that, you'll be in a better position to recruit the right employees for your team.

The first step in creating that team, before you do anything else, is to define what it is you must achieve. Break down your goals, as precisely as you can, into the steps you'll have to take to reach them, and then identify the skills necessary to take each step. Finally, match those skills up with individuals who can bring them to your team.

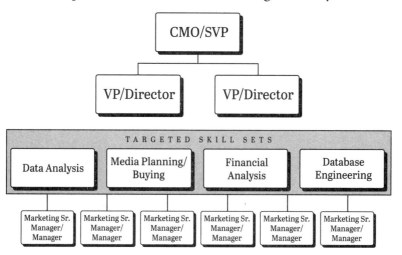

You're still going to require videographers and graphic designers and people who can write creative content, but you're also going to need data analysts and software engineers, as well as people who know about SEO optimization and people with social media and mobile experience. You may require people who can build apps and understand cloud capabilities or have a background in operations research. People with a tech background and people with an accounting background will also be necessary, as well as folks with a traditional marketing background. Given the language barrier between tech people and marketing people, you also want to make sure you have "translators" on the team, people who comprehend customers and business needs but speak the language of IT, and technical people with a strong understanding of marketing campaigns and the business side. You'll require business-solution architects who can help you put data together and organize them so that they're ready to analyze. These are people who know how to structure data so it can be activated. In essence, they are data translators. You also want statisticians and data scientists who can communicate their knowledge to nonexperts. In short, you want individuals who will bring a whole bunch of skills to your table, but they should have one thing in common: they get excited about learning new things. They adapt easily to new challenges and new ways of doing things. They're agile.

"When I think about hiring the right marketing team, I can't help but think about the Fantastic 4. While individually they would fail to take down the evil villains they constantly face, together they work as an amazing unit because they utilize each other's skills."

—A.J. Grawal, CEO, *Alumnify*[127]

This means that when you sit down to interview your applicants, you're going to care a lot less about which schools they went to and a whole lot more about their ability to think outside the box (or better yet, know that a box even exists). When I'm interviewing, I tend to ask questions such as "How many soccer balls would it take to fill up this room?" "How many gas stations do you think there are in town?" I'm not so much looking for a right answer as I am looking for someone who can engage intelligently with the question. If applicants blurt out a quick answer, I usually cross them off my list. I'm not really looking for *the* answer but instead someone who knows how to think through *the* problem.

I'm looking for people who have a lot of flexibility, who can change priorities, who are multiskilled. I don't want to hire a one-trick pony. The more skills I can bring into my team, the more agile and dimensional my team will be. Most of all, I want people who are good problem solvers and who are also comfortable with being accountable to what the data is saying. In my opinion, that's more important than having someone on the team who has lots of exclusive experience with building and executing marketing campaigns.

"Building a strong and diverse team is critical when delivering big results. The best-run departments or teams have diverse skills and backgrounds and tend to operate as a unit not as individuals. When you have a team with the similar skill sets and backgrounds, they tend to think in a jar and operate as individuals focused on achieving their own goal delivering the organization smaller results."

—David Sobel, partner, CEO Coaching International

A truly agile team can deliver whatever is necessary in a given situation. Sometimes that might be creativity. Other times it's tech innovation. Sometimes it's data analysis, or it could be all three at once. If you have a team of cuttlefish marketers, you can deliver whatever is required for the immediate circumstances at hand. You don't have to place an order and wait for delivery. You already have whatever it is you need, right there where you can grab it when you need it. That's agility. And that's an effective team.

Remember, though, that your role is what makes or breaks a good team. Let's say you've built the most agile, innovative, broad-skilled marketing team in the world, but you're not willing to change how you lead. If you can't get out of your own way, you won't be a cuttlefish marketer. The cuttlefish marketer truly takes advantage of each strength available to it. That requires an entirely different mind-set from old-style marketing leadership. On the one hand, as we've said already, you must totally own the big picture, and on the other hand, you must be willing to let go of your personal preferences and become accountable to data feedback. This style of leadership provides direction while allowing the team room to respond quickly to market changes and consumer feedback.

> *"If you change yourself you will change your world. If you change how you think then you will change how you feel and what actions you take. And so the world around you will change. Not only because you are now viewing your environment through new lenses of thoughts and emotions but also because the change within can allow you to take action in ways*

you wouldn't have—or maybe even have thought about—while stuck in your old thought patterns."

—Henrik Edberg[128]

DO IT AS DORITOS DOES

The marketing executives at Doritos have demonstrated this new agile leadership style. For the past ten years, Doritos has invited the general public to take part in competing for the chance to promote its chips. The company's marketing executives ask for totally original, thirty-second commercials, and the winning ad gets a Super Bowl commercial spot, which is worth upward of $5,000,000 of media.[129] The Crash the Super Bowl campaign has generated a new level of loyalty from Doritos' customers. The opportunity to feel engaged with the company gives fans a sense of involvement and excitement that drives sales. Doritos' Crash the Super Bowl campaign required an unusual level of confidence from its marketing leaders, a willingness to let go while still holding on—loosening the reins, as it were, all while driving the company's growth to new levels.

Now, companies are taking the same crowdsourcing methodology Doritos uses and applying it internally. Using employees as the crowd to uncover new products, ideas, and solutions doesn't only engender employee loyalty and engagement; it also gives marketing executives access to the creative ideas of a much larger group of people. Their teams' boundaries are expanded.

Adam Siegel, the CEO of Cultivate Labs, points out in a recent CEO.com article that this methodology has massive benefits. "Individuals can advocate for what they believe is best for the company . . . [which] turns employees into motivated, problem-solving intrapreneurs." Siegel goes on to say that "companies often struggle with how to best prioritize resources and constantly ask themselves, 'Are we working on the right things?' Crowdsourcing means companies get a powerful signal about which ideas to work on from the people who know best."[130]

Siegel has several recommendations for making this methodology work. Even if you decide that internal crowdsourcing is not for you, his advice applies to team building in general in today's marketing world. First, Siegel says, the new approach to team involvement should feel organic, not like something that's forced from the top down. This goes back to what I said earlier: you can't try to shape new-style marketing teams using old-style leadership methods. Along the same lines, Siegel adds that, as the marketing leader, you must guide and provide incentive without taking over. You shouldn't let your personal biases get in the way of your team's power. "Get out of the way," Siegel says.

> *The hardest, most important part of this process is clearing the path for people to work on their ideas . . . driving innovation can't just be talk. Carve out time in your employees' days so they can work on their ideas.*
>
> *Although this may be something new for your organization, it should ultimately be thought of as a permanent change—a method that simply becomes the way you do business. Have fun getting your whole team involved, and remember to bring a bag of Doritos for snacks.[131]*

"Invest in 'students.' No, I'm not suggesting you scour the local high schools or colleges for budding marketing talent. What I mean is that you should hire people who are dedicated to learning."

—Joanna Lord, VP of Marketing, Porch[132]

CREATING INNOVATIVE TEAMS

Siegel suggests applying the 5x5 framework from MIT Sloan School of Management's Professor Michael Schrage in order to encourage innovation; give diverse teams of five people five days to come up with five business experiments that cost no more than $5,000 each and take no longer than five weeks to run.[133] This is a very agile methodology, one that Schrage insists must be accountable to data.

Schrage's book, *The Innovator's Hypothesis,* isn't directed specifically toward marketing teams, but since his ideas about innovation are meant to foster hypergrowth businesses, they apply equally to marketing departments. As top executives build their teams, he says, they must have the "discipline and courage" to emphasize three things:

1. What are our innovation objectives? What do they want their innovation impact to look and feel like? What does innovation success look and feel like? This needs to be explicitly discussed and defined and shared. Everyone needs to understand this.

2. What are the innovation behaviors we are trying to create and encourage? Do our incentives reflect that? Innovation isn't just the ideas and hypotheses in people's heads; it's the experiments and prototypes and interactions we have with our customers and each other. What are our commodity innovation behaviors? What are our unique behaviors?

3. What innovation capabilities are we cultivating in our people? Are we training people to design experiments and hypotheses, not just educating them? We need to view innovation not just as a business process but as a collection of individual and social capabilities. The more

capable our people, the more innovative they will be. That means more value.[134]

What I like about Schrage's concept of innovation is that it goes a step further than creativity. His ideas speak to the creativity-versus-data issue we talked about back in chapter 4. You don't want to build a team that focuses on "good ideas," Schrage says. Instead, you want to "insist your people think, communicate, and design around testable hypotheses."[135] If you can build a team culture that's focused on testable hypotheses, you're encouraging objective creativity that's accountable to data. You're turning the art of marketing into the science of marketing. As a cuttlefish marketer, you want a team made up of people with varied skills, who work together within a culture of innovation.

"The skills that make someone a great PR leader capable of spinning up the next big story are entirely different from the visual designer who's going to create a killer new website, which is different than the marketing ops ace who's going to implement the latest campaign attribution technology. CMOs need to tailor their management styles to lead and inspire a diverse group of marketers to be their best."

—Scott Holden, CMO, ThoughtSpot[136]

CUTTLEFISH TEAM BUILDING

The Old Spice Guy, the Oreo tweet, the Dancing Pony, Doritos' Crash the Super Bowl ad campaign—all these are amazing success stories in the marketing world. But the real success stories are the marketing executives who bred, believed in, and managed a team culture where amazing, agile, data-based creativity could thrive and evolve.

We're all finding our way in this new marketing world. The big agencies are struggling to build their teams just as much as marketing directors are. Publicis, an agency-holding company, recently bought the technology company Sapient. The enormous agency Digitas has formed a joint working group with Oracle, a very large tech company. Agencies such as Publicis and Digitas are desperately trying to figure out how to evolve the concept of the agency partner team. One thing is certain: anyone who wants to build a marketing team that will thrive in today's world is going to have to think outside the old boxes.

If you or I had been asked to design an efficient ocean predator, we probably wouldn't have come up with a cuttlefish. You might say that the cuttlefish is a good example of evolutionary, outside-the-box thinking and coming up with a collection of surprising strengths and unexpected abilities that work together successfully. When we build our teams, we want to do the same. We want to create groups of people who can function together as hypergrowth businesses do; who work with IT as an integrated nervous system; who respond to data as organically as a cuttlefish does to light; and who can work under a new style of management.

We want agile cuttlefish marketers.

"Don't think about buying titles—think about buying outcomes. Think about plugging gaping holes in the company. Are you signing up customers so fast that you can't respond to all the support emails?

> *Don't hire a head of support, hire someone that helps you tackle the support issue. Someone that's maniacally committed to customer happiness."*
>
> —Dharmesh Shah, CTO, HubSpot[137]

KEY POINTS TO REMEMBER

→ Your successful marketing team is no longer made up of a bunch of people with marketing degrees. Instead, it takes the wide range of skills that make teams agile in today's fast-paced market.

→ Data provides information that enables you to choose people with the skills you truly require.

→ You want a team of individuals who understand the new world of marketing, people who are agile, IT savvy, and data driven.

→ Before you do anything else, define what it is you need to achieve, identify the skills necessary for each step, and match those skills up with individuals who can bring them to your team.

→ You can't shape new-style marketing teams using old-style leadership methods.

CONCLUSION

THE FOCUSED, MODERN, MARKETING EXECUTIVE

We've talked a lot about the cuttlefish's incredible visual abilities. But here's the thing: cuttlefish are colorblind—or at least they should be. They have rod cells (the retina cells that are sensitive to light), but they lack the cone cells our eyes have to perceive color, which means cuttlefish should only be able to perceive black and white.[138]

When scientists realized this, they were mystified. Cuttlefish depend on color to hunt and communicate. They respond to the slightest change of coloration in their environments, and they put on amazing displays of color and pattern across their skin. So how can they possibly not be able to see color?

As it turns out, cuttlefish can't see color in the way we do, but they *can* detect it. The father-and-son research partners Christopher and Alexander Stubbs recently discovered that cuttlefish's incredible ability to adjust their visual focus is what allows them to "see" color in a way that's totally different from ours. According to Alexander Stubbs, "This is an entirely different scheme than the multi-color visual pigments that are common in humans and many other animals. "These organisms seem to have the machinery for color vision, just not in a way we had previously imagined."[139]

We tend to think of objects as having fixed colors—an apple, for example, is red, and its leaves are green—but in reality, color is the result of the way in which the object reflects and absorbs light. And as we've already said, the cuttlefish is an expert when it comes to detecting and understanding light data.

The key to the cuttlefish's color perception is its long, W-shaped pupil, which allows light to enter the eye from many directions. Whereas our pupils contract to give us sharper vision, cuttlefish eyes have evolved to take in as much light as possible, from as many angles as possible. This causes what's known as chromatic aberration, the colorful fringes we sometimes see around things when our eyes are bleary. We see these blurred edges as a problem, as something that interferes with "normal" vision, and we work to prevent chromatic aberration from happening in camera and telescope lenses. Cuttlefish, however, actually accentuate chromatic aberration, using that fringe of color to understand their environment in ways we can't begin to comprehend. They may not be able to "see" colors the way we do, but they definitely understand light.

Stubbs explains that it's the cuttlefish's unique focal powers that allow it to do this. Its entire eyeball can actually change in depth in order to increase or decrease the distance between the lens and the retina, while its pupil can move back and forth—in a way that looks quite disconcerting to those of us who have pupils that are fixed in the center of our irises—allowing light to slant in from as many directions as possible.[140]

If our eyes were to suddenly start behaving like this, our brains wouldn't be equipped to handle it. Based on that experience, we'd probably conclude that cuttlefish vision is so unfocused and blurry that the poor creatures might as well be blind. But obviously that's not the case. Instead, their focal powers far exceed our own, picking up incredibly detailed light data that their brains use to create perceptions that are sharper than we can begin to imagine. "Intriguingly," Stubbs says, "using chromatic aberration to detect color is more computationally intensive than other types of color vision, such as our own, and likely requires a lot of brainpower." [141] This may explain, in part, why these creatures are the most intelligent invertebrates on Earth. It's also what allows them to be such incredibly successful predators.

As cuttlefish marketers, we too must have a version of these qualities: focal power and intelligence. As we create and lead departments equipped with a "lens" to let in a wide range of data, there's the potential for all that data to blur our understanding. The sheer amount of data can obscure rather than clarify our comprehension. Our task is to bring that data into focus to make sense out of it, to put it together in a way that gives us sharply detailed images of our marketplace, allowing us to achieve new levels of success.

FINDING OUR FOCUS

Patrick Spenner, the strategic initiatives leader for CEB Marketing, has claimed that "the distinctive trait of winning marketing functions will be their focus." [142] Spenner tells the story of a head of marketing whose team had conducted dozens of digital champion-challenger tests in a year that led to a $4 million boost in marketing efficiency and effectiveness. Spenner points out that a lot of time and energy went into those digital tests, time and energy that could have been used to reduce the company's web page load time on its product websites. A one-second-faster web load would have translated into more than $10 million in business lift.

"This is the sort of organizational dynamic that only CMOs and their lieutenants can spot because they have the bird's eye view across all marketing activities," Spenner explains. "The individual marketer doing some of those A/B tests is optimizing her own world, yet can't see what that means for the bigger picture of marketing." He concludes that stories like this "highlight the real, underlying risk—loss of focus on what really moves the needle for the business—for marketing leaders amid a consumer landscape frenzied with change."[143]

I've talked a lot in this book about the necessity for CMOs to own the big picture and all the parts that contribute to that, including IT, data, outside partnerships, and teams. Owning the big picture is only possible when we have the focus to clearly see it. Otherwise, we'll simply be confused by all the moving parts. Focus is what will give us clarity and direction so that we can lead.

This big-picture focus comes from a firm foundation in accountability to data.

This big-picture focus comes from a firm foundation in accountability to data. But I also believe there's a certain degree of artistry involved. You could say, "Look, this can all be done programmatically, using an algorithm. I don't need an artist to tell me that this media should cost $13 when the marketplace, based upon dynamic, is telling me it should cost $6. Where's artistry in that?" But data alone won't give us the focus we must have. We require cuttlefish-brain ability to put the data together and then act on it.

> *"While keeping the plates spinning for the marketing operation will still be core to the role [of CMO], a relentless focus on spotting opportunities to innovate to create brand growth matters more and more."*
>
> —Omaid Hiwaizi, President of Global Marketing, Blippar[144]

TRAIT #1: BE AGILE

We need the cuttlefish's amazing ability to adapt quickly and creatively to the demands of whatever is going on around us. Instead of an automatic set of responses we trot out again and again, we want to demonstrate the intelligence and active choice of a cuttlefish's predatory skills. We don't merely act quickly; we truly *respond* in the sense that our actions are generated by outside stimuli, a swift and immediate reaction to circumstances that integrate into everything we do, as are the cuttlefish's actions. This rapid responsiveness is inherent in marketing's overall function. It's the essential skill that pulls everything together. It's what makes the marketing department's function integral to the entire life force of a hypergrowth business.

From the perspective of software engineering, agility means rapid and adaptive response to change, effective communication among all stakeholders, drawing the customer onto the team, and organizing a team so that it is in control of the work performed. Agility is driven by customer demand; it recognizes that all plans are short lived, so it develops ideas iteratively rather than with a final version in mind and with multiple increments to reach the final goal;

and it adapts as changes occur. When we apply this to marketing, agility becomes the speed at which we can adjust our processes to identify and deliver customer value—and make more money for the company. Marketing agility isn't the speed at which we execute a campaign; it's the speed at which we determine the best action over and over and over. Customer value is the goal of everything we do—producing anything that is not valuable to the customer is a waste of our time—and we can reach our goal more efficiently by making tiny, incremental shifts in our marketing rather than huge course adjustments. Learning from what works and what doesn't work, using data, we continuously improve. This agility requires responsive IT that gives us the ability to access the right information at the right time—information derived from well-activated data that gives us accountability and transparency. It also requires that we take the initiative within our professional partnerships rather than outsourcing leadership, and it requires that we choose teams with the necessary skills to act quickly.

As marketing executives, we should see our function as integrated with the entire business. Our priorities must be the same as those of the overall business: building rapid growth. We are directly responsible for our company's profitability, and we must embrace other business operations to do this.

With the world changing so quickly, our job as marketers is to keep up, not fall behind and become obsolete. We cultivate versatility and flexibility. We are willing to let go of tradition to be responsive to the present—and the future. We take over the market and outstrip our competitors when we respond swiftly and agilely to customer demands. As are cuttlefish, we are so engaged with the world around us that we can sense and respond to stimuli fast enough to drive the most appropriate result for the environment's or market's demands.

The digital revolution has made reading the market a fundamental skill that is a must for all successful marketing directors. It requires the qualities of a hypergrowth business: a rigorous analysis of consumers' needs, careful mapping of the competitive landscape, and the ability to precisely define what makes our own company different from all others, uniquely able to satisfy our customers. In today's world, the customer is always the one who dictates the direction the company must take. Anything we map out ahead of time must be easily changed and adapted; our plans must be fluid and flexible. It's not just a matter of responding quickly to changes in the marketplace; we're also coming up against competitors who are doing the same thing. Countless players—from our competitors to politics, new tech developments to world events—are all interacting at once. Since we never know what might happen between the time we have an idea and the time we execute it, we'd have to be flexible. If we're not agile and fast, we won't be able to respond quickly enough to whatever happens. We'll be caught by surprise, and we may be left behind as a result.

Running our marketing department as though it were a hyper-growth business requires a new set of personal skills. We must be flexible and adaptable. We must let go of our inclination to be in control. We can't insist that we're always right. Instead, we must adjust quickly to new situations as they arise. We must quickly let go of ideas that don't work and try something new. We must have enough objectivity and humility to let the marketplace drive our decision making. And we must have enough personal energy to keep going, continually thinking and rethinking, always fine-tuning everything we do rather than letting the momentum of the status quo carry us forward. We must use all the skills at our disposal and power through. We can't hesitate or go slow, because we lack self-confidence. At the same time, a dash of healthy paranoia—the awareness that there are countless factors that could work against us—can help us stay energized.

TRAIT #2: DIRECT YOUR TECHNOLOGY

The cuttlefish's rapid responses rely on its nervous system picking up accurate messages from the environment, carrying those messages to the brain, and then sending out instantaneous responses to the entire body. IT functions in a similar way for modern marketing, despite the traditional disconnect and communication breakdowns between IT and marketing departments. In a world where the Internet is both a significant market in itself and a way to engage and understand customers, the accuracy, speed, and precision of IT systems mean the difference between winning and losing customers. This means that marketing executives must leverage technology to improve customer experience and drive sales growth. To do this, we must make use of our tech departments for web- and data-based marketing activities, such as the use of analytics tools that allow us to connect data on channels, technologies, social media outreach, ads, and offers; conversion optimization to get people to come to our websites—and then do what we want them to; basic communication functions such as customized e-mail campaigns; search engine marketing, using ads and SEO; remarketing using web display ads; mobile phone adaptations and apps; and marketing automation that brings it all together, from analytics to online forms, from customer tracking to personalized website content, from e-mail campaigns to automated alerts to sales people.

Because today's agile marketing is so integrated with IT, both use some of the same vocabulary and methodologies, especially those pertaining to Scrum: short bursts of marketing campaigns called sprints that are based on planning, daily scrums (fifteen-minute mini-meetings), and then reviewing the sprint before moving on to the next one. This agile software methodology can be an extremely effective tool for cuttlefish marketers.

This reliance on IT methodologies and input can feel uncomfortable simply because we're not accustomed to it. We must let go of all our old ideas about marketing people and IT people being drastically different from each other and unable to speak the same language. Instead, we must learn to function in harmony, synergistically. For modern marketing directors, managing marketing departments increasingly means managing and influencing IT as well. Marketing and technology no longer live in separate silos. Now they're a single symbiotic organism. They must creatively interact continuously to produce innovative customer experiences in complex environments that are intensely competitive.

This doesn't mean we marketers should understand complicated coding and other high-end IT functions. But we do need to grasp the bigger IT picture so that we can make sure that our team is building the right platforms for scalability, flexibility, and all the other things required by both IT and marketing. We can no longer think of IT as something separate from everything else we do. We must be able to direct its essential and organic functions within our departments. New advances in technology will shape our marketing strategies, and our marketing strategies will guide where and how we invest in tech. Then, as we use technology, it will help us to refine and reshape our strategies, creating an ever-turning cycle that will keep us innovative, agile, competitive, and constantly growing in response to our markets.

Coordinating all these processes is an enormously complex task that requires a big-picture perspective—our perspectives as marketing directors—to fit together all the pieces. That doesn't mean we should go back to school and get an engineering degree, but we should learn enough to be engaged and actively involved so that we can give direction. Our team members are the ones closest to IT's practical requirements, so as marketing directors, we should be the ones who drive efficient development.

TRAIT #3: ACTIVATE DATA

In the same way that cuttlefish don't merely collect light data—for them, data collection and instant response are inseparably linked, allowing them to be successful predators—we must cultivate an ongoing sensitivity to data. A cuttlefish's nervous system would do it little good without a system for collecting information from its environment, and in a similar way, our IT is only as effective as the data we feed into it. Our departments should be as organically linked to data as a cuttlefish is. Relying on data can't be regarded as an add-on to the marketing process any more than technology can be. Data is what empowers us, giving us the information we require to be flexible and fast. When we activate data, embracing transparency and accountability, we become cuttlefish marketers, learning fast and moving fast.

Focusing on the wrong data, however, is nearly as bad as having no data. Although everyone knows that we have more data at our disposal than ever before. We must *activate* that data, actually deriving meaningful insights from it and converting it into action. One of the most important ways to do this is to define specifically what our goals are so that the IT department knows exactly what it is we're looking for.

This data not only offers statistical analysis but also behavioral data and social media analysis that marketing and sales departments can use to discover answers to specific questions. Marketing departments can now study multiple, co-occurring buyer behaviors based on past purchases to predict future buying behaviors. Social monitoring analytics, for example, can be applied to the same information that buyers are exposed to through blogs and social media. Marketing teams have access to countless meaningful insights into who is talking about their products, what they are saying, and what and who is influencing them. This customer data is collected via billions of connected devices, creating a constantly surging tide of data that is not only immense in volume but also moves at a breakneck speed. If marketing departments can't respond equally fast, the information will be useless because it will already be out of date or the opportunity has passed. Marketing data offers insights into which content is the most effective at each stage of a sales cycle; provides the foundation for strategies for increasing conversion rates, prospect engagement, and revenue; and allows companies to optimize their pricing strategies. Most of all, though, marketing data gives us what we must have to create a new form of customer engagement.

Data collection is not an extra activity that will make us better marketers. As a cuttlefish's light sensors are essential to its existence, so is data collection technology essential to companies' existence. It's a constant and ongoing process that is integrated into everything we do, the ever-present basis for how we navigate within our markets, a fluid stream of information that is never the same from one day to the next. There is no final answer. Because the world is constantly changing at an ever-increasing pace, data will change as well. We must be flexible, willing to go with the flow, creating cultures of transparency and accountability to data.

Within a corporate culture of accountability and transparency, it's not just the executives who use data; it's everyone inside the organization and external agency and vendor partners. If everybody in the organization has access to the same information executives do, monthly and quarterly readouts will become obsolete because they'll be replaced by real-time discussion. This level of transparency can feel uncomfortable, but a culture like this makes sure the entire company has access to information by distributing reports and talking about them, regardless of whether the data indicates success or failure. We must stop feeling threatened by negative data and begin to understand that negative data is just as useful as positive data. When we do this, we can define success differently than we have in the past. Success doesn't mean we get everything right the first time. Instead, success means embracing negative data and then jumping on it to turn around the things that aren't working. Failure needn't discourage us. And we don't want to feel defensive and point fingers in response to failure. Instead, a culture of transparency and accountability allows us to learn fast, change fast, and act fast. We can discuss openly the things that don't work—and why. Together, we can find a way to learn and improve. We create an environment that allows for failure and use it as an opportunity to build even greater success.

Data also should not be seen as the enemy of creativity. As marketing directors, we claim ownership of both sides—both creativity and data—in order to build the big-picture perspective. Our job is to steer our departments by owning data so that we can lead and direct objective creativity. We are the ones who direct the big-picture perspective. Whenever we look at data, we want to be the ones who decide what the takeaway is.

We facilitate putting all the data pieces together, linking together a wide variety of data sets in order to paint a complete picture of the customer. Then we turn this coherent customer data picture into a source of new value, using behavioral segmenting to understand what subgroups within our customer base will respond best to which media. We understand predictive analytics, deciding which portfolio of products we should emphasize to different groups of customers.

All this new customer data doesn't mean we no longer require old-fashioned, traditional data, such as revenue versus expenses, net income, and so on. Instead, as marketing executives, we look at data as a triangle, where our time is divided between three angles. In the first angle—one-third of our time—we focus on monitoring and tracking our company's fundamental health in terms of revenue and expenses (and how marketing contributes especially to the bottom line). The second angle of the data triangle—another third of our time—focuses on marketing efforts that the data says are working. We should understand why they're working and how we can build on them in new ways to create more success. The final angle of the triangle—and another third of our time—has to do with all the marketing that the data indicates isn't working. This last third of our time is spent looking at why these things aren't working and what we can do to improve them. Keeping this triangle in mind as we interact with data will help us balance our time and energy. We don't want to be too focused on any single angle of the triangle. We should keep all three angles active and engaged.

TRAIT #4: DON'T OUTSOURCE YOUR LEADERSHIP

As cuttlefish marketers, we don't outsource our leadership or our thinking. This doesn't mean we can't leverage agencies and outside consultants, but we don't want to sit back waiting for everyone else to take care of things. We want to be the one in charge. We own the relationship in the same way we own our IT and our data. We communicate clearly from a position of active involvement in everything that's going on. Otherwise, with one agency handling one thing, another something else, and yet another agency doing something else for our company, if we're not responsible for the overall big picture, that picture will soon become fragmented. As marketing executives, we are the ones who see the big-picture goals, and we must be the ones who integrate everything to reach those goals. All elements of a business's cost chain—including both production and marketing—should be understood and optimized. To do this, we must think about our relationships with outside agencies in a new way, as a new kind of partnership.

We want to be sure we're getting what we pay for whenever we work with outside agencies. Waste is one of the potential major flaws of huge agencies with massive overheads that drive expenses higher. Instead, we want to build partnerships of highly specialized experts. We also want to be sure that we're avoiding kickback arrangements between agencies and media outlets, and we don't want to assume that by working with big agencies we'll benefit from a trickle-down network effect. When we're directing the big picture, rather than outsourcing our thinking and leadership, we're in position to sort through the agencies out there and form relationships with the ones that will offer us the most expertise for particular marketing tasks. We should think of agencies as assets to maximize return, not as magic bullets to solve all our problems and do our thinking for us. Rather than hiring a single company to be our brain, we focus on matching the best providers with our individual requirements. When we're already in position to reach out to partners with the right skill sets, we have more flexibility to react as the needs of particular campaigns unfold. Our job is to keep everything on target, focused on the overall goals. We do this by reviewing our existing agencies' performance and choosing carefully before we create new relationships.

At the same time, though, we must have an effective working relationship with our outside partners, one that's based on good communication that's adapted to the requisites of our partners. As cuttlefish marketers, we understand that what works in one setting doesn't always work in another, and we're willing to adapt to new demands.

We also don't try to outsource our customers' trust to our agency partners. The digital world fosters genuine and immediate contact between brands and their users, and agencies can't fake on our behalf that level of true engagement.

Agencies and other outside vendors bring real value to our marketing. We must find productive ways to outsource some aspects of our work, and it makes sense to make use of all the resources out there to supplement our own. But at the end of the day, as the marketing directors, we must make the calls. We can't outsource our responsibility to be the brain that runs the entire show.

TRAIT #5: BUILD A DIFFERENT KIND OF TEAM

Just as the cuttlefish's array of peculiar traits creates a powerful and effective predator, we too must bring together a team that can function with the cuttlefish's level of agility and efficiency. The cuttlefish marketer should build a team that's different from the old-style marketing team, one that includes people with a wide range of skills and abilities. The first step toward creating that team, before we do anything else, is to define what we seek to achieve. If we break down our goals as precisely as we can, we'll be able to identify the skills necessary to achieve each objective that will lead us to our goals. Once we've done that, we can match those skills with the individuals who deliver them. We'll still need people to deliver creative content, but we will also require data analysts and software engineers, people with tech backgrounds, accounting backgrounds, and operations research backgrounds. We want individuals who will bring us all the skills that will enable us to be cuttlefish marketers. We want people who will adapt easily to new challenges and new ways of doing things.

We use data to look at people's track records to create agile teams that can deliver whatever is necessary in a given situation, whether that's a crazy and creative idea, a tech innovation, data analysis, or a combination of all three. Cuttlefish teams can deliver whatever is required for the immediate circumstances at hand. They already have whatever is needed as situations arise. That's what makes them so agile.

As the leaders of these teams, we're responsible for keeping the data and creativity integrated. We not only build teams that produce good ideas but also bring together people who keep their creativity objective, constantly accountable to data. We build a culture of innovation that's based on data, and in doing so, we create teams that know how to turn the art of marketing into the science of marketing.

As marketing executives, our role is what makes or breaks our teams. Even if we've put together a team that has every possible agile skill we could ever imagine, if we can't get out of their way and let them function, they'll be unable to function at their potential. As cuttlefish marketers, we implement each strength on our teams. We own the entire big picture, and at the same time, we let go of our egos and become accountable to data feedback. Our job is to provide direction while allowing our teams the freedom to be agile, responsive, and effective.

ARTISTRY

I just watched a video of a cuttlefish catching its prey. The video starts with a floating creature looking a little like a luminescent, white prickly pear that's wearing a sleepy cartoon face. Its ruffly fin constantly ripples around its circumference, but otherwise, it is still, hovering a few inches above the bottom of the sea. It looks calm, harmless, and funny. And then there's a flicker of a fish in the background—and suddenly that pearly-looking cucumber of a creature is just . . . gone. In its place is something smooth, sleek, and dusky-gray, shaped like a dirigible, with two long purple arms reaching out on each side. It darts toward the fish . . . its tentacles shoot out of its mouth . . . then, just like that, the fish is sucked into its mouth and swallowed.

And now, the comical, white creature with its big nose and sleepy eyes floats once more in front of the camera.

That moment when the cuttlefish catches its prey is the moment when everything comes together: its agility in the water, its efficient nervous system, its sensitivity to light data, its centralized brain power, and its amazing multiple body parts all working together, all focused on a single purpose. It's the moment of artistry when, somehow, the sum is greater than all the parts added up separately.

Turning to my other favorite analogy—sports—think about the baseball pitcher. Can you break down his performance into stats? Yes, you can. Can you use science to analyze his pitch in terms of momentum and velocity and biomechanics? Absolutely. And all that's great. But ultimately, when all is said and done, the pitcher simply executes the pitch. Sure, he's using all that science, but in the moment that he pitches the ball—well, that's artistry. He's not thinking about the data at that moment. He's deploying it.

According to Mark Galley, the CEO of the behavioral marketing engine Zaius, that element of artistry is what we too must have. "Today's creative CMO needs to be so on top of the possibilities in order to think big and get creative across all channels."

In my mind, being "on top of all the possibilities" means we take all the elements of the cuttlefish marketer—the agility of a hyper-growth business, integrated technology, activated data, new kinds of partnerships, and well-built teams—and we bring them all into focus. And then, in that moment when an Oreo tweet, an Old Spice Guy dialogue, or a Dancing Pony video goes out into the world, everything comes together. It's not about just being creative or doing something new and innovative; it's about doing something new that *works*. That's what it means to be a cuttlefish marketer.

> *"As channels, time, business goals and customers change, CMOs need to be the ones . . . [that] can wrap up the entire organization and say, 'This is where the customer is supposed to head.'"*
>
> —Liz Miler, Senior Vice President of Marketing, CMO Council[145]

ENDNOTES

1   Mary Bates, "Why Do Chameleons Change Colors?" *Wired,* April 11, 2014, https://www.wired.com/2014/04/ how-do-chameleons-change-colors/.

2   Dave Hansford, "Cuttlefish Change Color, Shape-Shift to Elude Predators." *National Geographic,* August 6, 2008, http:// news.nationalgeographic.com/news/2008/08/080608-cut- tlefish-camouflage-missions.html.

3   "The Marlboro Man," *Advertising Age,* March 29, 1999, http:// adage.com/article/special-report-the-advertising-century/ marlboro-man/140170/.

4   Quoted in "5 Marketing Lessons from Old Spice," by Dave Smith. *Inc.,* August 18, 2011, http://www.inc.com/ articles/201108/5-marketing-lessons-from-old-spice.html.

5   "Case Study: Old Spice Response Campaign." D&AD, 2016, http://www.dandad.org/ en/d-ad-old-spice-case-study-digital-marketing/.

6   360i, "360i Report: The CMO's Guide to Big Data," November 25, 2014, http://blog.360i.com/ web-design/360i-report-cmos-guide-big-data.

7   360i, "Red Roof Inn Traffic-Tracking Technology," accessed September 15, 2016, https://360i.com/work/ traffic-tracking-tech/.

8   Walmart, "Walmart Announces New Search Engine to Power Walmart.com," Walmart.com, August 30, 2012, http:// corporate.walmart.com/_news_/news-archive/2012/08/30/ walmart-announces-new-search-engine-to-power-walmart-com.

9   Steve Dee, "How Does Capital One Differentiate Itself in the Card Industry?" *Forbes*, September 11, 2015, http:// www.forbes.com/sites/greatspeculations/2015/09/11/ how-does-capital-one-differentiate-itself-in-the-card-industry/#55a4577b1edc.

10 Larry Paige, "111 Motivational Business Quotes," Severn. com.

11 Liz Froment, "Marketing and Big Data," Zembula, September 11, 2015, http://www.zembula.com/ blog/20-quotes-marketing-big-data/.

12 Hansford, "Cuttlefish Change Color, Shape-Shift to Elude Predators."

13 Shelley A. Adamo, Kelly Ehgoetz, Cheryl Sangster, and Ivy Whitehorne, "Signaling to the Enemy? Body Pattern Expression and Its Response to External Cues During Hunting in the Cuttlefish *Sepia officinalis* (Cephalopoda)," *Biological Bulletin,* June 2006, 192–200.

14 Simon Johnstone, "What Is Marketing Agility in Action?" Marketing Operations Partners, September 28, 2015, http://mopartners.com/what-is-marketing-agility-in-action/.

15 Matt Stratz, "Does Branding Need to Be Rebranded?" *The Makegood,* May 15, 2012, http://www.the-makegood.com/2012/05/15/does-branding-need-to-be-rebranded/.

16 "Innovation, Research and Development: A Dyson Case Study." Business Case Studies, May 2016, http://businesscasestudies.co.uk/dyson/innovation-research-and-development/#axzz4JQS3aORv.

17 Johnstone, "What Is Marketing Agility in Action?"

18 Roger Pressman, *Software Engineering: A Practitioner's Approach,* (New York: McGraw-Hill, 2009), chapter 3.

19 "What Is Marketing?" The Chartered Institute of Marketing, 2016, http://www.cim.co.uk/more/getin2marketing/what-is-marketing/.

20 Joel York, "What Is Marketing Agility?" Markodojo, December 8, 2015, http://www.markodojo.com/what-is-marketing-agility/.

21 Ibid.

22 Patrick Hanlon, "If Sir Dyson Doesn't Believe In Brands, Why Has He Spent Millions Building One?" *Forbes,* May 6, 2012, http://www.forbes.com/sites/patrickhanlon/2012/05/06/if-

sir-dyson-doesnt-believe-in-brands-why-has-he-spent-milli-ons-building-one/#57746384559f.

23   Matthew Creamer, "James Dyson: 'I Don't Believe in Brand.'" Advertising Age, May 2, 2012, http://adage.com/article/adages/design-icon-james-dyson-i-brand/234494/.

24   Michael Hiltzik, "Kodak's Long Fade to Black," latimes.com, December 4, 2011.

25   Richard Branson, "Change," Virgin.com, February 6, 2015, https://www.virgin.com/richard-branson/my-top-10-quotes-on-change.

26   "Facts and Statistics on Apple." Statista, 2016, https://www.statista.com/topics/847/apple/.

27   Diego A. Comin and Martí Mestieri, "Technology Diffusion: Measurement, Causes and Con0sequences." The National Bureau of Economic Research, May 2012, NBER Working Paper No. 19052, http://www.nber.org/papers/w19052.

28   Pamela Vaughn, "Shelf Life of Social Media Links Only 3 Hours [Data]," HubSpot, September 8, 2011, http://blog.hubspot.com/blog/tabid/6307/bid/24507/Shelf-Life-of-Social-Media-Links-Only-3-Hours-Data.aspx#sm.00009xn yhpgq7equ10qc7sftga0o3.

29   Kevan Lee, "The Social Media Frequency Guide: How Often to Post to Facebook, Twitter, LinkedIn, and More," Buffer, July 4, 2014, https://blog.bufferapp.com/social-media-frequency-guide.

30   Stephen Levy, "A Brief History of the Eniac Computer," Smithsonian, November 2013,

http://www.smithsonianmag.com/history/
the-brief-history-of-the-eniac-computer-3889120/?no-ist.

31 "Your Smartphone Is Millions of Times More Powerful That All of NASA's Combined Computing in 1969," ZME Science, accessed October 2, 2016, http://www.zmescience.com/research/technology/ smartphone-power-compared-to-apollo-432/.

32 Mark Schaefer, "Content Shock: Why Content Marketing Is Not a Sustainable Strategy," January 6, 2014, http://www. businessesgrow.com/2014/01/06/content-shock/.

33 Shelly Lucas, "Marketing Agility: The Missing Metric?" Dun & Bradstreet, September 30, 2016, http://www.dnb.com/ perspectives/marketing-sales/marketing-agility-measure-ment.html.

34 Anna Isaac, "The 10 essential qualities of a modern marketer," *The Telegraph,* July 28, 2016, http://www. telegraph.co.uk/connect/media-and-technology/ ten-qualities-modern-marketers-must-have/.

35 Ibid.

36 Steve Benna, "17 Mark Cuban Quotes on What It Takes to Run a Business," Inc., September 21, 2015, http://www.inc. com/business-insider/17-best-mark-cuban-quotes.html.

37 Patrick Spenner, "The Rise of the Marketing Entre-preneur," *Forbes,* January 26, 2012, http://www. forbes.com/sites/patrickspenner/2012/01/26/ the-rise-of-the-marketing-entrepreneur/#3de5ec813384.

38 Elizabeth Preston, "Cuttlefish Can Count," *Discover,* September 1, 2016, http://blogs.discovermagazine.com/inkfish/2016/09/01/cuttlefish-can-count-to-five/#.V-VR3JMrIXo.

39 Clint Boulton, "IT and marketing collaborate to sweeten websites for digital natives," CIO, March 22, 2016, http://www.cio.com/article/3047040/cio-role/it-and-marketing-collaborate-to-sweeten-websites-for-digital-natives.html.

40 Ibid.

41 Scrum Guides, http://www.scrumguides.org/.

42 Andrea Fryrear, "Guide to Using Scrum Methodology for Agile Marketing," Marketer Gizmo, March 5, 2015, http://www.marketergizmo.com/guide-to-using-scrum-methodology-for-agile-marketing/.

43 Elena Varon, "Agility In Action: How Four Brands Are Using Agile Marketing," CMO, May 20, 2013, scl.io/ltgqjj7p#gs.dzxhBEQ.

44 Ibid.

45 Jeroen Molenaar, "Marketing scrum vs IT scrum—two marketing case studies," Xebia Netherlands, July 15, 2014, http://blog.xebia.com/marketing-scrum-vs-it-scrum/.

46 Christian Friedrich Hornschuch, quoted in Nina Lovering Marshall's *Mosses and Lichens: A Popular Guide to the Identification and Study of Our Commoner Mosses and Lichens, Their Uses, and Methods of Preserving* (New York: Doubleday, 1919), 22.

47 Bill Bryson, *A Short History of Nearly Everything* (New York: Broadway, 2006), 423.

48 Adobe, "Why marketing and IT need to get along better," *Business Insider*, September 30, 2015, http://www.businessinsider. com/sc/better-relationship-for-it-and-marketing-2015-9.

49 Scott Brinker, "Strategy, marketing, and technology are all intertwined," ChiefMarTech.com, January 20, 2014, http://chiefmartec.com/2014/01/ strategy-marketing-technology-intertwined/.

50 Damien Cummings, "The problem with agencies & tech vendors: They don't understand the business of marketing," Digital Future, September 19, 2015, http://damiencummings.blogspot.com/.

51 Ibid.

52 Ibid.

53 Scott Brinker, "Marketing Technology Landscape Supergraphic (2016)," ChiefMarech.com, March 21, 2016, http://chiefmartec.com/2016/03/ marketing-technology-landscape-supergraphic-2016/.

54 Adobe, "Why marketing and IT need to get along better."

55 Brian Ferrario, "Why Agencies Should Be Betting on Big Data," Drawbridge, August 4, 2016, https://www.drawbridge. com/news/p/why-agencies-should-be-betting-big-on-data.

56 S.E. Temple, V. Pignatelli, T. Cook, M.J. How, T.-H. Chiou, N.W. Roberts, and N.J. Marshall, "High-resolution polarisation vision in a cuttlefish," *Current Biology*, February 21, 2012, http://dx.doi.org/10.1016/j.cub.2012.01.010

57 Froment, "Marketing and Big Data."

58 Maeve Hosea, "Why transparency in data is key to building trust," *Marketing Week,* June 15, 2016, https://www.marketingweek.com/2016/06/15/ why-transparency-in-data-is-key-to-building-trust/.

59 Ibid.

60 Ibid.

61 Froment, "Marketing and Big Data."

62 Ibid.

63 "Trident Marketing Increases Revenue Nearly 1,000 percent with Predictive Analytics" (Somers, NY: IBM Corporation, 2012).

64 Ibid.

65 Elana Varon, "Agility In Action: How Four Brands Are Using Agile Marketing," CMO, May 20, 2013, scl.io/ltgqjj7p#gs. yy4VNxM.

66 Jason Peaslee, "Case Study—GE and Big Data," Thrive Analytics, May 7, 2013, http://www.thriveanalytics.com/ blog/?p=15.

67 Germain Lussier, "How Much Internet Bandwidth Does Netflix Use?" *Film,* March 28, 2015, http://www.slashfilm. com/netflix-bandwidth-usage/.

68 "Walmart Launches New Mobile Apps to Give Customers Better Shopping Experiences Online and In-Store," Walmart.com, November 1, 2011, http://www.walmartlabs. com/press-releases/walmart-launches-new-mobile-apps-to-

give-customers-better-shopping-experiences-online-and-in-store/.

69   Froment, "Marketing and Big Data."

70   "How companies are using big data and analytics," McKinsey & Company, April 2016, http://www.mckinsey. com/business-functions/mckinsey-analytics/our-insights/ how-companies-are-using-big-data-and-analytics.

71   Hosea, "Why transparency in data is key to building trust."

72   Louis Columbus, "Ten Ways Big Data Is Revolutionizing Marketing and Sales," *Forbes,* May 9, 2016, http://www.forbes. com/sites/louiscolumbus/2016/05/09/ten-ways-big-data-is-revolutionizing-marketing-and-sales/#f1290b3115eb.

73   Froment, "Marketing and Big Data."

74   Ibid.

75   Matt Ariker, Martin Harrysson, and Jesko Perrey, "Getting the CMO and CIO to work as partners," McKinsey & Company, August 2014, http://www.mckinsey.com/ business-functions/business-technology/our-insights/ getting-the-cmo-and-cio-to-work-as-partners.

76   Nadia Goodman, "James Dyson on Using Failure to Drive Success," *Entrepreneur,* November 5, 2012, https://www. entrepreneur.com/article/224855.

77   Ibid.

78   Michael Barnett, "Data vs. Creativity," *Marketing Week,* April 10, 2013, https://www.marketingweek.com/2013/04/10/ data-vs-creativity/.

79   Lara O'Reilly, "Three launches Fleetwood Mac dancing horse ad," *Marketing Week,* March 1, 2013.

80   Stephen Dahl, *Social Media Marketing: Theories and Applications* (New York: Sage, 2014).

81   Barnett, "Data vs. Creativity."

82   "The Internet Is for Dancing Ponies, in Campaign for Brit Mobile Network Three," *Advertising Age,* March 1, 2013, http://adage.com/article/creativity-pick-of-the-day/internet-dancing-ponies-campaign-brit-mobile-network/240118/.

83   Stephanie Overby, "A Digital Dozen: 12 Traits of the Truly Creative CMO," CMO.com, July 25, 2016, http://scl.io/RD1c0irD#gs.CminTCs.

84   John Snyder, "Creativity and Data: The New 21st Century Paradigm," Huffington Post, February 22, 2016, http://www.huffingtonpost.com/advertising-week/creativity-and-data-the-n_b_9290340.html.

85   Ash Bendelow, "Data vs creativity? Data should be a huge tool in the ongoing fight against mediocrity," The Drum, October 27, 2014, http://www.thedrum.com/opinion/2014/10/27/data-vs-creativity-data-should-be-huge-tool-ongoing-fight-against-mediocrity.

86   CMO Summit Survey, "2016 CMO Summit Survey Highlights," Spencer Stuart, April 2016, https://www.spencerstuart.com/research-and-insight/2016-cmo-summit-survey-highlights.

87   Ferrario, "Why Agencies Should Be Betting on Big Data."

88 Jess Nussbaum, "Data's Place in the Growing AdTech Marketplace Ecosystem," Dun & Bradstreet, September 22, 2016, http://www.dnb.com/perspectives/marketing-sales/datas-place-in-the-adtech-marketplace-ecosystem.html.

89 B.B. Boycott, "The Functional Organization of the Brain of the Cuttlefish *Sepia officinalis*," *Proceedings of the Royal Society, Biological Sciences*, February 28, 1961, 10.1098/rspb.1961.0015.

90 Alexandra Bruell, "Agencies, Marketing-Tech Companies on Quest for Personalized Content," Advertising Age, February 9, 2016, http://adage.com/article/agency-news/agencies-marketing-tech-giants-team-perfect-personalized-marketing/302537/.

91 Ibid.

92 Ibid.

93 Ibid.

94 Lindsay Stein, "Future for Agencies and Clients Will Focus on Partnerships," Advertising Age, September 27, 2016, http://adage.com/article/agency-news/future-agencies-clients-focus-partnerships/306051/.

95 Ibid.

96 Ibid.

97 Gary Milner, "The End of Advertising, as We Know It," *Media Daily News*, July 23, 2016, http://www.mediapost.com/publications/article/280953/the-end-of-advertising-as-we-know-it.html.

98 Ibid.

99 Ibid.

100 Alexandra Bruell, "Media-Agency Kickbacks. Yes, They're Real," Advertising Age, March 23, 2015, http://adage.com/ article/agency-news/media-agency-kickbacks-real/297707/.

101 Ibid.

102 Ibid.

103 Jessica Wohl, "Agencies, You're on Notice: Your Clients Are Likely Prepping for Reviews in the Coming Year, Survey Finds," Advertising Age, September 29, 2016, http://adage.com/article/agencies/thirds-top-advertisers-plan-reviews/306077/?utm_source=agency_email&utm_medium=newsletter&utm_campaign=adage&ttl=14758680 17?utm_visit=1642811.

104 Rae Ann Fera, "Revealing The Naked Truth Behind the Agency-Client Relationship," Fast Company, June 26, 2014, https://www.fastcocreate.com/3032321/cannes/revealing-the-naked-truth-behind-the-agency-client-relationship.

105 RPA, "New Advertising Industry Survey Reveals How Trust Between Advertising Agencies and Clients Leads to Creative Success," RPA.com, June 18, 2014, http://www.rpa.com/ press/2014-06-18-naked-at-cannes/.

106 Ibid.

107 Ibid.

108 A. C. Crook, R. Baddeley, and D. Osorio, "Identifying the structure in cuttlefish visual signals." *Philosophical Transactions of the Royal Society of London B: Biological Sciences*, 2002, 357 (1427): 1617–1624. doi:10.1098/rstb.2002.1070.

109 M. E. Palmer, M. R. Calvé, and S. A. Adamo, "Response of female cuttlefish Sepia officinalis (Cephalopoda) to mirrors and conspecifics: evidence for signaling in female cuttlefish," *Animal Cognition*, 2002, 9(2): 151–155. doi:10.1007/s10071-005-0009-0.

110 S. A. Adamo and R. T. Hanlon "Do cuttlefish (Cephalopoda) signal their intentions to conspecifics during agonistic encounters?" *Animal Behaviour*, 1996, 52(1): 73–81. doi:10.1006/anbe.1996.0153.

111 P. Hutton, B. M. Seymoure, K. J. McGraw, R. A. Ligon, and R. K. Simpson, "Dynamic color communication," *Current Opinion in Behavioral Sciences*, 2015, 6: 41–49. doi:10.1016/j.cobeha.2015.08.007.

112 A. Thomas, C. MacDonald, "Investigating body patterning in aquarium-raised flamboyant cuttlefish (Metasepia pfefferi)," *Peer Journal*, 2016, 4: e2035. doi:10.7717/peerj.2035.

113 R. T. Hanlon, M. J. Naud, P. W. Shaw, and J. N. Havenhand, "Behavioural ecology: transient sexual mimicry leads to fertilization," *Nature*, 2015, 433(7,023): 212–212.

114 Ibid.

115 Fera, "Revealing The Naked Truth Behind the Agency-Client Relationship."

116 David Garland, "5 Predictions on the Future of Marketing, PR and Advertising Agencies," The Rise to the Top, September 2016, https://therisetothetop.com/davids-blog/5-predictions-future-marketing-pr-advertising-agencies/.

117 Nova, "The Anatomy of a Cuttlefish," PBS, accessed September 25, 2016, http://www.pbs.org/wgbh/nova/camo/anat-nf.html.

118 Neale Monks, "A Broad Brush History of the Cephalopoda," The Cephalopod Page, accessed October 1, 2016, http://www.thecephalopodpage.org/evolution.php.

119 Dharmesh Shah, "15 Brilliant Business Lessons from Moneyball," LinkedIn, January 15, 2013, https://www.linkedin.com/pulse/20130115162356-658789-19-brilliant-business-lessons-from-moneyball.

120 Overby, "A Digital Dozen: 12 Traits of the Truly Creative CMO."

121 Jennifer Rooney, "Behind the Scenes of Oreo's Real-Time Super Bowl Slam Dunk," *Forbes,* February 4, 2013, http://www.forbes.com/sites/jenniferrooney/2013/02/04/behind-the-scenes-of-oreos-real-time-super-bowl-slam-dunk/#6966e06f59ee.

122 Jim Edwards, "Oreo's Super Bowl Power-Outage Tweet Was 18 Months in the Making," *Business Insider,* March 12, 2013, http://www.businessinsider.com/oreos-super-bowl-power-outage-tweet-was-18-months-in-the-making-2013-3.

123 David Kaplan, "Oreo's 'Overnight Success' In Social Media Was 100 Years in the Making," Ad Exchanger, March 12, 2013, http://adexchanger.com/social-media/oreos-overnight-success-in-social-media-was-100-years-in-the-making/.

124 Rooney, "Behind the Scenes of Oreo's Real-Time Super Bowl Slam Dunk."

125 Iain Tait in an interview with Mark Borden, "The Team Who Made Old Spice Smell Good Again Reveals What's Behind Mustafa's Towel." FastCompany, July 14, 2010, http://www. fastcompany.com/1670314/team-who-made-old-spice-smell-good-again-reveals-whats-behind-mustafas-towel.

126 Adam McKibbin, "The Future of IT-Marketing Collaboration," iMeet Central, January 5, 2016, http://imeetcentral.com/the-future-of-it-marketing-collaboration.

127 A. J. Agrawal, "3 Strategies for Building a Successful Marketing Team," November 25, 2015, http://www.inc.com/aj-agrawal/three-strategies-for-building-a-successful-marketing-team.html.

128 Henrik Edberg, "Gandhi's Top 10 Fundamentals for Changing the World," The Positivity Blog, accessed October 1, 2016, http://www.positivityblog.com/index.php/2008/05/09/gandhis-top-10-fundamentals-for-changing-the-world/.

129 Nick Schwartz, "Stunning Infographic Charts the Skyrocketing Cost of a Super Bowl Ad," For the Win, February 6, 2016, http://ftw.usatoday.com/2016/02/how-much-does-super-bowl-ad-cost.

130 Adam Siegel, "Do It Like Doritos: Use Crowdsourcing Inside Your Company To Find Your Best Ideas," CEO.com, May 17, 2016, http://www.ceo.com/operations/do-it-like-doritos-use-crowdsourcing-inside-your-company-to-find-your-best-ideas/.

131 Ibid.

132 Joanna Lord, "5 Tips for Hiring an All-Star Marketing Team," *Entrepreneur*, March 11, 2013, https://www.entrepreneur.com/article/226002.

133 Jimmy Gutterman, "Michael Schrage on Why Experiments Are So Much Better Than Ideas," Collective Next, March 5, 2015, http://www.collectivenext.com/blog/michael-schrage-why-experiments-are-so-much-better-ideas.

134 Ibid.

135 Ibid.

136 Overby, "A Digital Dozen: 12 Traits of the Truly Creative CMO."

137 Shah.

138 Marine Biological Laboratory, "Cuttlefish Masters of Disguise Despite Colorblindness," *Science Daily*, April 20, 2006, https://www.sciencedaily.com/releases/2006/04/060419072340.htm.

139 "Study proposes explanation for how cephalopods see color, despite black and white vision," Phys.org, July 4, 2016, http://phys.org/news/2016-07-explanation-cephalopods-black-white-vision.html.

140 Robert Sanders, "Weird pupils let octopuses see their colorful gardens," *Berkeley News*, July 5, 2016, http://news.berkeley.edu/2016/07/05/weird-pupils-let-octopuses-see-their-colorful-gardens/.

141 Ibid.

142 Patrick Spenner, "The Surprising Key to Market Agility," *Forbes*, March 16, 2012, http://www.

forbes.com/sites/patrickspenner/2012/03/16/
the-surprising-key-to-marketing-agility/#4b45e2c650d3.

143 Ibid.

144 Overby, "A Digital Dozen: 12 Traits of the Truly Creative CMO."

145 Jim Williams, "Want to Be a Successful CMO? 4 Skills You Need to Have," Influitive, September 29, 2015, http://influi-tive.com/blog/want-to-be-a-successful-cmo-heres-4-skills-you-need-to-have/.

CUTTLEFISH DRAWINGS